THE TOV HEART

God's Design *for a* Life Rooted *in* What Matters Most

RAY SCHMIDT

Copyright © 2025 Ray Schmidt

Published by Invested Stories LLC

All rights reserved, no part of this publication may be reproduced, stored in a retrieval system, or transmitted in any form or by any means—electronic, mechanical, photocopy, recording, or any other—except for brief quotations in printed reviews, without the prior permission of the author.

All Scripture quotations, unless otherwise indicated, are taken from the Holy Bible, New International Version® NIV®. Copyright ©1973, 1978; 1984; 2011 by Biblica, Inc.® Used by permission of Zondervan. All rights reserved worldwide. www,zondervan.com. The "NIV" and "New International Version" are trademarks registered in the United States Patent and Trademark Office: by Biblica, Inc.®

Scripture quotations marked NLT are taken from the Holy Bible, New Living Translation, copyright ©1996, 2004, 2015 by Tyndale House Foundation. Used by permission of Tyndale House Publishers, a Division of Tyndale House Ministries, Carol Stream, Illinois 60188. All rights reserved.

Scripture quotations marked ESV are from the ESV® Bible (The Holy Bible, English Standard Version®), © 2001 by Crossway, a publishing ministry of Good News Publishers. Used by permission. All rights reserved.

Scripture quotations marked MSG are taken from THE MESSAGE, copyright ©1993, 2002, 2018 by Eugene H. Peterson. Used by permission of NavPress. All rights reserved. Represented by Tyndale House Publishers, a Division of Tyndale House Ministries.

The following are registered trademarks of Invested Stories LLC – Tov Heart; Alive, Full, Free; God Math

Printed in the United States of America

ISBN: 978-0-9986240-6-8 (print)
ISBN: 978-0-9986240-7-5 (Kindle/ePub)

First Edition 2025

Cover design by Kristen Ingebretson, penmeetpaper.com
Layout by Lorie DeWorken, mindthemargins.com

DEDICATION

For the thirsty.
Men who want more.

"... let us move beyond the elementary teachings about Christ and be taken forward to maturity, not laying again the foundation of repentance from acts that lead to death, and of faith in God, instruction about cleansing rites, the laying on of hands, the resurrection of the dead, and eternal judgment. And God permitting, we will do so."

Hebrews 6:1-3

CONTENTS

Introduction 1

PART ONE: FROM SLOW DEATH TO ABUNDANT LIFE
Chapter 1: Slow Death 9
Chapter 2: Choosing Life 17

PART TWO: THE HEART OF EVERYTHING
Chapter 3: Awareness of the Difficult 41
Chapter 4: Finding Your Way 59
Chapter 5: Unconsidered Ascents 77

PART THREE: DISCOVERING GOD'S TOV HEART
Chapter 6: God the Gardener 101
Chapter 7: Sowing Tov 117

PART FOUR: AWAKENING THE TOV HEART
Chapter 8: God Math 141
Chapter 9: Farming Tov 181

PART FIVE: GUARDING THE TOV HEART
Chapter 10: Required Nourishment 201
Chapter 11: Understanding the Opposition . . . 215
Chapter 12: Belayed & Belaying 235

PART SIX: EPILOGUE
Chapter 13: Reprise 263

APPENDIX: GOING DEEPER   273

Notes 277
Acknowledgments 286
About the Author 287

INTRODUCTION

*"Ask and it will be given to you;
seek and you will find; knock and the door
will be opened to you. For everyone who asks
receives; the one who seeks finds; and to the one
who knocks, the door will be opened."*

JESUS OF NAZARETH
MATTHEW 7:7-8

STILL ON THE JOURNEY

Junah: *"Bagger, you're one hell of a caddy."*

Bagger: *"Well, I do the best with what I've got to work with."*[1]

My journey with God has been a lot like how I play golf: Many good shots. Some awesome. Quite a few shots into the woods, over the green, into the sand, and, well...twenty yards from the tee box...in almost every direction. It's what we used to call "diagonal golf."

I've lost a lot of balls over the years. I've scored ten over par on a single hole. I have also made a hole-in-one.

So, I keep coming back. I keep playing. And you know what? I get better.

For most of my life, I walked with God dogged by fear. I've gone from a young, fatherless boy in Sunday School memorizing Luke 2:10-12 to a man in mid-life collapse, both personally and professionally, and finally to a man on a personal journey of restoration and redemption. A journey of the heart through fear to abundant life.

But don't misunderstand me—I am still on this journey, and abundant life is not perfect life. At least not in the sense that all my circumstances are, well, perfect. Yes, I have come a long way, but I still have a long way to go. And I still live in a fallen world, a world where, as Jesus said, "you will have trouble."

I am a quote guy, which means I use quotes of all kinds to illustrate and clarify. A favorite for me to keep front and center is from a book by Mary Stewart called *The Last Enchantment*.[2] "However much folks knows there's always someone as knows more." I know, the language is a bit strange. But simply put, no matter how much you think you know, someone else always knows more.

It's clear, I still have much to learn. A lifetime's worth and beyond.

But I am intimately aware that you and I live in a world bereft of true life. Something is missing, and we can't quite put our finger on it.

Before *The Fall of Man*[3] God created a garden where everything was Tov. Usually translated into English as "good," the Hebrew word tov means so much more than simply good. In the Garden of Eden life flourished and everything God created was able to fulfill both its design and purpose in creation. Life that brought forth more life. Exponentially.

At the Fall, the world was introduced to disobedience and rebellion. We lost everything we had in the Garden of Eden. Most importantly we lost our union with God. We lost true life and the environment where that life flourished.

Ever since, every human being has been trying to find their way back.

"And we've got to get ourselves back to the garden."[4]

If you're like me, your journey "back to the Garden" started when you fell in love with Jesus. Then you were told to serve, tithe, step in, and step up because that is how you would find the life you were looking for, what it means to be a Christian.

The truth is most of those we follow in the church don't know how to live life abundantly. Not really.

As my friend Tim Hayes puts it,

> *You can participate in corporate worship, serve in your church, memorize Bible verses, practice spiritual disciplines, master doctrinal understanding, even be an honest-to-God born-again person, yet miss out on the lion's share of life with Jesus. Those things are all good and even helpful on the journey of life with Jesus, but they can also be practiced for the sake of practice.*

Most of us practice what we practice for the sake of practicing. But Jesus made life in the Kingdom, life with him, abundant life, very simple.

> *"But seek first his kingdom and his righteousness, and all these things will be given to you as well."* – Matthew 6:33

Simple, yes. Easy, not so much. At least not as easy as our twenty-first-century, neo-evangelical selves would like it to be.

The abundant life Jesus promised is an adventure, and adventures can be dangerous, taking us into wild and unknown territory.

> *"It's a dangerous business, Frodo, going out your door. You step onto the road, and if you don't keep your feet, there's no knowing where you might be swept off to."*[5]

To find abundant life, you must be willing to be swept off your feet. To follow Jesus wherever he leads. No matter where, no matter what, no matter how. Whether you understand or not, and especially when the outcome is unclear.

There are two things I want to reiterate as we step out the door.

- *That there is more to Tov than being "good" and,*
- *That you can only trust Jesus through a heart redeemed and restored.*

Tov means much more than "good." More than pleasant or satisfying or beneficial. When something is tov it is completely capable of fulfilling its design and purpose in creation.

To live abundantly you must trust Jesus. No matter what. But to truly trust him you will need a new heart. A heart redeemed and a heart restored. A heart oriented toward union with God as Adam's was in the Garden before the Fall.

You will need the Tov Heart.

FINDING THE WAY

"This is what the Lord says: 'Stand at the crossroads and look; ask for the ancient paths, ask where the good way is, and walk in it, and you will find rest for your souls.'" - Jeremiah 6:16a

As you traverse most trails in the wilderness there are markers that let you know the way to go. Whether it's a trail marked by man, or one marked by nature. These trail markers let you know that you are on the right path. Some may be easy to see and understand, some may be nuanced and hidden. But, whether nuanced or brightly colored, the path ahead is defined.

At the beginning of each section within a chapter, I have provided brief summaries that I am calling Tov Markers. If you wish, you can just scan the Tov Markers and catch the main point of each section. Choosing where and when to dive into the "meat" of each section as desire pulls and time allows.

While it is possible to grasp the main points of each section by reviewing the Tov Markers, I encourage you to dive into the nourishment to be found in the detail. Remember, God is in the details!

> *"The Lord directs the steps of the godly. He delights in every detail of their lives. Though they stumble, they will never fall, for the Lord holds them by the hand."* – Psalm 37:23-24 NLT

PART ONE

From Slow Death to Abundant Life

CHAPTER 1
SLOW DEATH

"Follow me, and let the dead bury their own dead."

JESUS OF NAZARETH
MATTHEW 8:22

SEARCHING FOR SOMETHING

"Any true life of the spirit must be narrated as a story of God's search for humankind, not humankind's search for God."
– Eugene Peterson, *Praying with the Psalms*[6]

TOV MARKER
We are all searching for something to bring us happiness, joy, hope, or peace. Most of us misidentify our something and, as a result, embrace distraction and medication. Wasting our most precious resource. Time.

We're all searching for something. Exactly what that something is depends on you. Who you've become and who you're becoming.

Both are strongly influenced by life with your family and your own personal experience of joy, sorrow, desire, dreams, success, failure, pain, and trauma. Who you've become is singular. A messy, sophisticated blend of these influences and your personal responses to them. The choices you make to sin or not in the face of temptation or another's sin around and against you.

Your something might be the "best." The best fishing hole, the best deer stand location, the best chainsaw, or the best golf course. It might be the best new book, the best undiscovered piece of art, the best video game, or the best new song. It could even be the best cheesecake, the best steak, or the best beer.

Your something could be the "next." The next job, the next spouse or girlfriend. The next vacation, the next adventure, or the next challenge or praise at home or at work.

Your something might simply be "relief." Relief from pain, boredom, fear, stress, or loneliness.

Your something is probably a mix of the above, plus some. But one thing is certain: your something is as diverse as it is old. As diverse as each man born into the world. And as old as the thirst that has haunted men for generation upon generation.

As King Solomon put it,

"What has been will be again, what has been done will be done again; there is nothing new under the sun." – Ecclesiastes 1:9

The futility and sadness underlying this verse almost make you want to give up the search. Almost. But your life depends on your "something" ...right?

Whatever your something is, the longer you've been searching for it, the more frustrating life becomes. And while you don't want to admit it, that something you're searching for has begun to drive the bus of your life.

If you're honest, your something has become subconsciously consuming. It consumes your thoughts, your actions, and your reserves. The result of this consumption is that your most precious resource, time, is squandered in the pursuit of it. It may start with "Walter Mitty"[7] daydreaming. But soon the search transitions to Google, Instagram, Facebook, Tik-Tok, or another darker "something" search engine.

What happens if we can't find our something? Oh, God help us if we can't find it!

We distract and medicate.

Between internet surfing, streaming services, online porn, the liquor store, and the neighborhood "illicit pharmaceutical salesman" the options for distraction and medication are endless.

We end up with distraction and medication because most often we misidentify our something. The something we long for is not a thing that makes us feel better but a way of being that brings us life. Spiritual not physical. The life we were created to live in the Garden. Life that is unperturbed by circumstances, good or bad. The life Jesus promised was why he came. Abundant life.

MY SEARCH

"It is strange but true that the most important turning points of life often come at the most unexpected times and in the most unexpected ways."
– Napoleon Hill[8]

TOV MARKER
There is more to walking with God. Unexpectedly more. If you will let him show you there is simply more.

In 2006, a group of men were putting on a local version of the *Wild at Heart Boot Camp* in southwestern Virginia. Their guest speaker was a member of the Wild at Heart team named Craig McConnell. Craig was gifted with a winsome manner that drew you in and made you believe you were seen and known. I met Craig at the Wild at Heart Boot Camp I'd attended in Colorado the year before. His story was similar to mine and I wanted to see if the acquaintance might develop into a friendship. Like most good men looking to make something happen I decided to make the five-hour drive and try to connect with Craig.

John Eldredge had just released his follow-up book to *Wild at Heart* called *The Way of the Wild Heart*[9] (later renamed *Fathered by God*[10]). I tend to be auditory in my learning, so I ordered a CD of the book to have something to listen to on the drive. Yes, this was BSS...Before Streaming Services.

Little did I know that God had different plans for me that weekend. It turned out that the trip wasn't about Craig, and it wasn't about the Boot Camp.

I barely connected with Craig that weekend, and I really don't remember much about the event itself. What I do remember is God getting me alone in a car for ten hours. Alone with this book, to set me on a journey that, at this point, I believe will take a lifetime. Not in the sense of a mountain too high to climb but in the sense of ever-increasing fullness of life. One of the most beautiful and exciting things about walking with God is that there is always more. More to know, more to experience, more to love. Simply more!

SOMEDAY

"Someday isn't a day of the week. It doesn't come around automatically. You gotta go out there and get it." – Emma Scott[11]

TOV MARKER
We all make plans for the future. For someday. For most of us, those plans never bear fruit. But, someday is here. Someday is now.

It is the journeys never started that we regret the most. I have had more than my share of journeys never started or started and never finished. To be honest, this book almost became one of them.

Tom Cruise and Jamie Foxx starred in the 2004 film *Collateral*.[12] It's the story of an assassin who uses an unsuspecting cab driver to chauffeur him around the city on his "rounds." Jamie plays the cab driver, Max, and Max has big dreams. He dreams of starting his own chauffeur company. High-end cars, high-end clientele. He has done all the research and planned out every detail. But he's never pulled the trigger. He's been planning for ten years and he's still driving a cab.

In the 2010 action, adventure, rom-com film *Knight and Day*[13] (again starring Tom Cruise; this time alongside Cameron Diaz), Cameron plays a "random" airline passenger, June, whom the spy, Roy, played by Tom, uses to smuggle a top-secret battery through airport security.

June has been to Kansas City to find parts for the 1966 Pontiac GTO her father began restoring. Now that he is deceased, she intends to finish it for her sister as a wedding present. Once on the plane Roy and June strike up a conversation. June talks about the GTO and how her father would take her and her sister to junkyards looking for parts.

> **June:** *"I used to think that, someday, when the last part went in, I would just climb into that GTO and start it up. Just drive and drive and drive, and just keep driving until I got to the tip of South America."*
> **Roy:** *"Yeah, 'someday.' That's a dangerous word."*
> **June:** *"Dangerous?"*
> **Roy:** *"It's really just code for 'never.'"*

Someday. "*Someday I will*_____." You fill in the blank. Start that company. Build that fence. Move to the country. Learn to sail. Open that store. Learn to play the guitar that's been sitting in the corner for twenty years. Take that risk. Write that book. Find God.

Today is *someday*, my friend. Someday is now.

CHAPTER 2
CHOOSING LIFE

"Now fear the Lord and serve him with all faithfulness.... But if serving the Lord seems undesirable to you, then choose for yourselves this day whom you will serve.... But as for me and my household, we will serve the Lord."

JOSHUA 24:14-15

THE WAY GOD WORKS

> *"Whatever else is going on, we can know this: God is always up to our transformation."* – John Eldredge, *Walking with God*[14]

TOV MARKER
God works in and through the holy and anointed. He also works in and through the simple and unexpected. The way God works and abundant life, are experienced through your restored heart. The tov heart.

During the 2020 pandemic, I was leading Zoom-based book studies. Mike and his wife joined me for one of these and, after the study, we stayed connected for about a year, then lost touch. Two years later, Mike reached out. The wheels had come off a good portion of his life. His marriage was good, but his health, sleep, and internal life were train wrecks. We decided to walk together for a season and see where God might lead.

As it turns out, Mike had also leaned into John Eldredge's book *The Way of the Wild Heart* about ten years earlier and God had ushered in some powerful healing through it. Now, as he was struggling, he sensed God asking him to revisit the themes of *The Way of the Wild Heart* and use the companion workbook as a guide.

I hadn't picked up *The Way of the Wild Heart* since my road trip with God twenty years before, but since Mike was revisiting it, I thought it would be helpful for me to join him.

I cracked the stiff pages open, and John Eldredge's opening words took me completely by surprise.

At the beginning of the Introduction, John shares a story of a family trip to Alaska's Chichagof Island. Their guide took them to the interior of the island, where grizzlies are known to feed. While the bears were sleeping on that hot day, their guide had something special for them to see:

> *Our guide led us to a trail of what seemed to be massive footprints, with a stride of about two feet between them, pressed down into the bog and making a path through it. "It's a marked trail," he said. A path created by the footprints of the bears. "This one is probably centuries old. For as long as the bears have been on this island, they've taken this path. The cubs follow their elders, putting their feet exactly where the older bears walk. That's how they learn to cross this place."*
>
> *I began to walk in the marked trail, stepping into the firm, deep-worn places where bears had walked for centuries. I'm not sure how to describe the experience, but for some reason the word holy comes to mind. An ancient and fearful path through a wild and untamed place. I was following a proven way, laid down by those much stronger and far more prepared for this place than me.*[15]

Holy. Ancient. Proven. *An ancient and fearful path through a wild and untamed place.* YES! That's it! I couldn't write a better description of where we are headed. What God has led me to in the writing of this book.

But we are not covering the same ground as John—the masculine journey. No, we are searching for another destination. But one that is no less elusive and perilous to find.

We are seeking the path to abundant life. The Life Jesus told us was why he came. The life the apostles speak of in their writings as the normal Christian experience. The life we've heard whispers of since we were children. The life we desperately desire and are searching for, but which always seems to belong to someone else and is just beyond our reach. The life that seems to slip through our fingers like water, sand, or air.

We don't speak of this life too loudly because we fear, as Marcus Aurelius said of Rome in the movie *Gladiator*, that if we speak of it too loudly, it will vanish like the morning fog. *"There was once a dream that was Rome. You could only whisper it. Anything more than a whisper and it would vanish; it was so fragile."*

But our fear is misplaced. The life we seek is not fragile, and instead of whispering we should be shouting it from the rooftops. For if the truth of it were known, we could not hold back the multitudes that would seek it out. It is strong. It is powerful. It is true! Most importantly, it is available!

Sometimes God works in very simple, loving, unexpected ways.

I walk on the beach many evenings and some mornings each week, and every time, God gives me at least one scallop shell.

I love scallop shells. They are my favorite. The variations in color and design are breathtaking and bring joy to my heart. So, I've come to look forward to finding whatever Jesus puts in my path.

One Saturday morning as I started my walk on the beach, BANG, right out of the box, literally within a few steps, there in front of me was a beautiful scallop shell. For no reason other than curiosity, I paused and asked Jesus, "Jesus, are you up to something? Is there something special you're telling me? Why scallop shells?"

Immediately, Jesus answered, "Because you like them."

I was dumbfounded. The creator of all that is—shells, the ocean, sand, wind, clouds, birds, fish, and yes, even me—gives me presents simply because I like them.

These are the moments that, as Luke so eloquently said of Jesus's mother, Mary, we store up as treasures in our hearts.[16]

For me, this was one of those heart-treasure moments. When the love of God moves from knowledge to experience. From intellectual assent to absolute certainty.

Abundant life is found in the holy, ancient, and proven. It is also found in the simple and unexpected.

The way God works leads through your heart. Your heart redeemed. Restored and recreated as God intended when he created you. The tov heart.

TOV AND YOUR HEART

"Surely your goodness and love will follow me all the days of my life."
- King David, Psalm 23:6

TOV MARKER

Tov is both how God created and what he created. Tov is how he created you and what he created – the core of your being – your heart. Through the tov heart you can live abundantly. Life that is fully capable of fulfilling both God's design and purpose in the world.

English is full of lame words. Words used to describe things from the ordinary to the fantastic. The word "good" is one of them. The word "good" can be used to describe everything from a cookie to sex.

Biblical Hebrew, the language of the Old Testament of the Bible, on the other hand, provides for a more expansive meaning and interpretation of words. More precise and significantly more alive. The Hebrew word *tov* is an example. It is usually translated into English as simply good. However, the word tov is full of both depth and breadth beyond being simply good as we've come to understand the word. The fullness of which is like the difference between knowing about a person, as you might from reading a biography "know" Abraham Lincoln or Julius Caesar, and truly knowing them, personally, intimately, by living in their home or having them as a close friend.

The first use of tov in the Bible is when God creates light.

> *"And God said, 'Let there be light,' and there was light. God saw that the light was good [tov], and he separated the light from the darkness."* – Genesis 1:3-4

God only calls light tov. This gives us a sense of the meaning of the word and how we are to understand the importance of light. It is only things that enable life that God calls tov. The things that he creates that enable life to flourish and bring forth more life are tov.

Plants create more plants. Animals, more animals. Ultimately, people create more people. Creation and re-creation. But not the creation of clones—the creation of ongoing, singular uniqueness.

Look at any living thing in the world. A white oak tree develops and scatters acorns that, when they find an environment where life can flourish, produce more white oak trees. But each new white oak tree, while similar to the original, is different from any other. Unique.

The same is true for humans. Even in the case of identical twins, those "identical" twins are singular and unique. Both physically, from DNA to fingerprints, and spiritually, from spirit to heart.

This is tov. Life begetting life. Similar yet singular. Life that flourishes. Life that is fully capable of fulfilling both its design and purpose in the world: the creation of more life. Life that flourishes and, at the same time, creates an environment where other life can flourish. Again and again, over and over.

> *"... it produced a crop—a hundred, sixty or thirty times what was sown."* - Jesus of Nazareth, Matthew 13:8

Tov is both *what* and *how* God created. What he created itself reproduces life—from one many. How he created bestows upon the world the environment required for that life to be nourished, grow, and mature. Tov is life bringing forth more life.

And because we are created in the image of God, tov is how he intends for us to live out his creation in and through our lives. In and through the creation of more life. Growing and flourishing. Allowing his abundance to fill us to overflowing. The result being environments around us where life can multiply and flourish. Environments that produce an exponential harvest.

THE TOV HEART

Contrary to modern thought, we don't live our lives through our minds. Our minds acquire, analyze, and process information. But it's not through the intellectual assent to information that we live.

We live in and through our hearts. Our hearts are where we hold all we consider most dear. Where our convictions, what governs our actions, are formed.

I said earlier that your "something" is as old as the thirst that has haunted men for generation upon generation. That thirst is in your heart, not your head. Your head tries to manage, adapt, and compensate for the thirst. But it is in your heart that the thirst exists, and it is through your heart that this thirst is expressed. But there's a problem.

Our hearts are broken. Shattered, really. The Hebrew word is *shabar*. Picture shell fragments on the beach or a piece of fine pottery after a ten-foot fall.

King David put it like this:

"You, God, are my God, earnestly I seek you; I thirst for you, my whole being longs for you, in a dry and parched land where there is no water." – Psalm 63:1

And John Eldredge, being more succinct, said, *"People are not primarily rational. People are primarily thirsty."*[17]

Tov, however, is the ultimate thirst quencher. Tov is the expression of abundance. Living water flowing into your heart, filling it to overflowing.

> "*Let anyone who is thirsty come to me and drink. Whoever believes in me, as Scripture has said, rivers of living water will flow from within them.*" – John 7:37-38

Not just flowing into you but flowing in such abundance that it overflows into the world around you. Healing, restoring, and renewing from tov in your heart.

This is why your heart matters to God, why Solomon says:

> "*Above all else, guard your heart, for it is the wellspring of life within you.*" – Proverbs 4:23 NIV 1984

Tov is the creation and recreation of life. Over and over, again and again. Creation that leads to a harvest. In you, those closest to you, and out into the world far beyond what your eyes can see, and your mind can know.

It is only through your recreated heart that you are truly able to live abundantly. Singularly unique in design and purpose. Able to fulfill that design and purpose through the recreation of life in and around you. Both physically and spiritually. This was God's intent in the Garden of Eden, his intent in creation, and his intent when he created you.

Unfortunately, there is no "tov switch" we can flip. Adam and Eve chose poorly. And living our lives in the resulting world has de-created us. To the point where we speak of the idea of tov with a sigh of resignation. And with the oft-used phrase "Wouldn't that be nice."

Tov doesn't just magically show up on your doorstep. Because of The Fall, you must fight for it. You must ask for it persistently. You must seek it above all things. And you must knock on every door that seems closed to you until you find it.

If you want to find abundant life, you must learn to live it out in and through who God intended when he created you. That is only done in and through the tov heart.

ENVIRONMENTS THAT FLOURISH

> *"The righteous will flourish like a palm tree, they will grow like a cedar of Lebanon; planted in the house of the Lord, they will flourish in the courts of our God. They will still bear fruit in old age, they will stay fresh and green, proclaiming, 'The Lord is upright; he is my Rock, and there is no wickedness in him.'"* – Psalm 92:12-15

TOV MARKER

Out of his love, God created environments where life could flourish. As a man, created in his image, it's your purpose too. To create environments where life can flourish.

Have you ever thought about your purpose? Of course you have. We all do. Purpose is a simple word with profound power and impact. Your purpose is not defined by your age or ability. But if you don't have it, you flounder. If you have it, you thrive.

It is no coincidence that Jesus used an agricultural parable to illustrate what is necessary. Dare I say essential for tov to exist.

As men created in the image of God, to find our own purpose, we must first look at God's purpose in creation. Starting our exploration with a question: Why did God create?

"We love because he first loved us." – 1 John 1:19 ESV

We find our purpose in and through God's purpose in creation: his love. Looking at the flipside, how did God first demonstrate his love? He created. Looking at the account of creation in Genesis 1 and 2, God demonstrated his love and our purpose not only by making living things. He also created an environment where that life could flourish. Not simply life as we have come to know and live it out. But life that flourishes, reproduces, and creates more life—tov.

> *"In the beginning, God created the heavens and the earth. The earth was without form and void, and darkness was over the face of the deep. And the Spirit of God was hovering over the face of the waters."* – Genesis 1:1-2

Initially, there was simply water. I say "simply water" not to diminish water but to emphasize its singular importance.

Water is the source of all life. Crucial to the survival of everything, from the simplest to the most complex forms of life.

Technically, water *"... acts as both a solvent and a delivery mechanism, dissolving essential vitamins and nutrients from food and delivering them to cells. Our bodies also use water to flush out toxins, regulate body temperature, and aid our metabolism."*[18]

Practically, we can only live about three days without it. It's pretty simple: without water, we die quickly. And so, God, in the beginning, first laid down the foundation of life, the foundation of tov: water.

God's second act of creation was light.

> *"And God said, 'Let there be light,' and there was light. And God saw that the light was good. And God separated the light from the darkness. God called the light Day, and the darkness he called Night. And there was evening and there was morning, the first day."* – Genesis 1:3-5

In his second act of creation God brought light into the world, defined the first day, and *"saw that it was good"*. As I said earlier, the Hebrew word translated here as "good" is tov.

God saw that what he had created was not simply good or pleasant in the modern sense of the word. But functional and fully capable of performing both his desire and purpose in creation. What God created was able to multiply, recreate, and create more life. Life that flourished. Tov.

On Day Two, God separated the waters by creating an expanse he called "sky." Notice that nothing new was created on Day Two. God used the second day of creation to define the space between the waters, what had already been created.

To ensure life could flourish, God established boundaries and defined the environment he was creating.

> *"And God said, 'Let there be a vault between the waters to separate water from water.' So God made the vault and separated the water under the vault from the water above it. And it was so. God called the vault 'sky.' And there was evening, and there was morning—the second day."* – Genesis 1:6-7

From here on out, God creates new things within the context of this tov framework. Things that enhance the environment and either enable it to flourish or fill it with life.

Dry ground and plants; sun, moon and stars; birds and sea creatures; land animals; and, finally, Man.

When God had completed his initial creation, he gave all he had created to Adam. And God told him, *"It's yours, Adam; I give it all to you. Take charge of it and care for it."* God demonstrated his purpose through his love in creation and he gave it away. He created not only life but also an environment where life could flourish. Where life, both physical and spiritual, could reproduce, multiply, and create more life. Tov for everything that breathes, grows, swims, flies, and walks. And, especially for Adam and Eve.

What does that mean for your purpose as a man?

You have been created for a purpose in the image of God. In its simplest form, your purpose is to create environments where life can flourish. Environments that are tov. Environments producing a harvest. One hundred, sixty, or thirty times what is sown. First for yourself. Then for your family and others around you in ever-widening circles of relationship.

GOD'S ABUNDANCE IS YOURS

"If then you are wise, you will show yourself rather as a reservoir than as a canal. For a canal spreads abroad water as it receives it, but a reservoir waits until it is filled before overflowing, and thus communicates, without loss to itself, its superabundant water. In the Church at the present day, we have many canals, few reservoirs."
– Bernard of Clairvaux[19]

TOV MARKER
We cannot contain the abundance of God. So, it overflows. If we allow it in, it will overflow. Creating life. Abundant life. First for you and then for others. This is the essence of tov.

The abundance of God is always on display. If we are willing to look down, it shows itself in every blade of grass, every flower, animal, and insect. If we look up, it is on display in the clouds, birds in flight, the moon, and the stars. God's abundance can be found in every person, in every painting and song, in every smile, and in every tear.

If we will look, we also find the abundance of God within us. The leap of the heart when we see our children or grandchildren. The anticipation of time spent with someone we love. The weight of the glory we experience in the face of death, pain, or trauma. And the peace that transcends all understanding.[20]

God pours his abundance into our hearts so that we can live the life Jesus intends us to live. His abundance creates tov and fills our hearts to overflowing and creates an environment within us where life can flourish. And not only within us but, in the overflow of his abundance, environments that flourish for those around us.

We cannot create abundance, and we cannot give away what we don't have. And, we cannot manufacture the overflow of abundance. Everything we do on behalf of others must flow from the supernatural abundance of what we allow God to pour into us. If not, we and those around us will quickly dry out to a crackling crunch.

I say "allow God to pour into us" because we have a choice. While it is God who creates and bestows abundance,[21] he will not, out of his great love for us, do anything against our will.

Love is not compelled if it is to be love and not coercion. So, we have a choice to make, the most important choice any of us will ever make. Will we allow God in? Will we allow him to create tov in our hearts through the abundance that he offers? The abundance that results in environments where life can flourish and overflow into the world.

If we say yes to tov and the abundance of God, life will overflow. It is out of the overflow of God's abundance and flourishing life within us that we create environments where life can flourish for those around us. Environments where life can flourish for our wives, if we're married. For our families and those closest to us. And then for the people around us as far as the ripples of our lives run.

> "The Messiah's banquet is for everyone who wants it, and it is not leftovers only, but so much abundance you gather leftovers in armfuls." – Blaine Eldredge, *The Paradise King*[22]

The true purpose of your life is this one thing: to create environments where life can flourish.

Still other seed fell on good soil, where it produced a crop—a hundred, sixty or thirty times what was sown. Whoever has ears, let them hear. But the seed falling on good soil refers to someone who hears the word and understands it. This is the one who produces a crop, yielding a hundred, sixty or thirty times what was sown. – Matthew 13:8-9, 23

In the Parable of the Sower, Jesus shows us the result of a seed planted in a flourishing environment.

It yields a crop a hundred, sixty, or thirty times more than was sown. Life that flourishes. Life to the full. Life that is fully capable of fulfilling both God's design and purpose in the world.

This is the essence of tov.

ABUNDANT LIFE

"The thief comes only to steal and kill and destroy. I came that they may have life and have it abundantly."
– Jesus of Nazareth, John 10:10 ESV

TOV MARKER
Abundant life is often misunderstood. To step onto the path to abundant life you must trust and obey Jesus. No matter what!

Jesus says he came that we might have life and have it abundantly. So, what is this abundant life Jesus came to give us? It's a good idea to get our heads and hearts around exactly what we're looking for before we try to find it, right? After all, if abundant life is the outcome we seek, knowing what it is will help us recognize it when it shows up.

Many people equate abundant life with eternal life. Life that never ends. While life that doesn't end is a resulting blessing of abundant life, they are not the same. It is not the length of life we are looking for, but the quality and substance of the life Jesus promised. Think about it for a moment: what would it look like to live your current life forever? If you're like me, that's a pretty scary thought, so there must be more.

Some view abundant life as never-ending blessing. Wave after wave of material benefit. Still others see abundant life as ongoing ease and simplicity.

Now those things sound pretty good, but didn't Jesus also say that *"in this world you will have trouble"*?[23] Trouble sure doesn't sound like blessing, ease, or simplicity to me. The apostle Paul tells us, *"I know what it is to be in need, and I know what it is to have plenty. I have learned the secret of being content in any and every situation, whether well fed or hungry, whether living in plenty or in want."*[24]

Paul lived out of Christ's abundant life, yet at times was in need, hungry, and in want.

So, what is the abundant life Jesus promised, and how do we find it? The way ahead is as ancient as it is challenging. The way is known, but in today's world the path has not been maintained, and so it is overgrown and easy to miss.

In Paul's letter to the Philippians, he tells them that he has learned the "secret of being content", at peace, assured.

So, what is Paul's secret?

Unfortunately, he doesn't provide any details in Philippians. He simply states that "*I can do all this through him who gives me strength.*"[25] Great thought, but what does it mean? How does Jesus give him strength?

To get more clarity, let's look at Paul's powerful prayer for those he dearly loved in Ephesus.

> *When I think of all this, I fall to my knees and pray to the Father, the Creator of everything in heaven and on earth. I pray that from his glorious, unlimited resources he will empower you with inner strength through his Spirit. Then Christ will make his home in your hearts as you trust in him. Your roots will grow down into God's love and keep you strong. And may you have the power to understand, as all God's people should, how wide, how long, how high, and how deep his love is. May you experience the love of Christ, though it is too great to understand fully. Then you will be made complete with all the fullness of life and power that comes from God.* – Ephesians 3:14-19 NLT

Paul prays that his beloved in Ephesus would know and experience the secret he has found.

First, that God, out of his unlimited resources, his abundance, would provide them with inner strength through his Spirit. Inner strength is not something we can generate ourselves. It is not something you can make happen. This inner strength is imparted, given by God out of his abundance through our union with him.

It is through this inner strength, imparted to you by God, that you are able to trust Jesus. But trust is a choice. You must choose to trust him. Notice that this is the only thing Paul tells the Ephesians to actually do: trust Jesus. Everything else is up to God.

Through your trust in Jesus, he comes and makes his home in your heart. Here Paul returns to the Eden imagery of nature. Alive, green, growing, created on purpose, for a purpose. To recreate itself, to flourish. *"Your roots will grow down into God's love and keep you strong."*

Most trees have a taproot that provides both nourishment and stability. The more fertile the soil, the deeper the taproot grows. This results in a healthier, more stable tree able to withstand infestations and storms. For some trees, the taproot grows down twice the depth of the height of the tree. For example, if a tree is ten feet tall, its tap root can be up to twenty feet deep!

Your "roots," your foundation, your anchor and source of nourishment will grow. Where? Down deep into the fertile soil of God's love. And the result? The nourishment and strengthening of the "tree" that is the tov heart. Making you strong and secure no matter the circumstances you face. And as you continue to grow, you are made complete in God's love by the life and power of God flowing into your life. Which then overflows into the world around you.

Jesus expressed it this way:

> "I am the vine; you are the branches. If you remain in me and I in you, you will bear much fruit; apart from me you can do nothing." – John 15:5

To find your way to abundant life, you must first and foremost trust Jesus. Sounds simple, right?

While trusting Jesus may be simple, it may also be the hardest thing you ever do. To trust Jesus, no matter what. Whether experiencing joy or sorrow. Whether hungry or well-fed. No matter what.

I can't leave our discussion of abundant life without saying a bit about obedience.

Obedience is one of those words to which we have a visceral reaction. Did you feel it in your gut when I said I wanted to talk about obedience?

We react that way because we just don't like others telling us what to do. We live in a culture, at least here in the West, that is self-centered and self-absorbed. We have become lone rangers. Dedicated to our own good, usually out of self-preservation.

For some of us, obedience was quite literally beat into us. So, I get it, your gut clenches and your heart recoils when the words "obey", or "obedience" are mentioned. I urge you to hang in there and hear me out. I assure you, in the Kingdom of God, obey is not a "four-letter word."

I am old enough to remember the chorus of an old hymn we used to sing in church:

"Trust and obey, for there's no other way
To be happy in Jesus, but to trust and obey."[26]

To be honest, when we sang that old hymn, I didn't really think about it much. It was just another song we sang in church. But as I continue my journey with God, I continue to marvel at the connections and links in Scripture.

> *"Does the Lord delight in burnt offerings and sacrifices*
>   *as much as in obeying the Lord?*
> *To obey is better than sacrifice,*
>   *and to heed [trust] is better than the fat of rams."*
> – 1 Samuel 15:22

If you trust Jesus, you must obey him. Your obedience is the proving ground of your trust. In the Kingdom of God, trust and obedience are the currency of abundant life. They are corollaries. You cannot obey without trust, and you cannot truly trust without being obedient.

> *"...Jesus said, 'If you hold to my teaching [obey], you are really my disciples.'"* – John 8:31b

There are two approaches to obedience. The one I grew up with in the church was born out of obligation. We were to obey God because of the obligation of the cross. We obey because we're supposed to. But obligation is a poor motivator and, as a result, obedience remained in my head and never reached my heart. When grounded in obligation, obedience often ends up manifesting itself as resentment. And resentment often turns into rebellion. In my case it was different, it became apathy. Less obvious than rebellion, generally unseen. And easy to hide, especially in the church.

As I walk with God in every situation of my life, I am finding a much better reason to obey him. I obey him and walk in obedience because I know, deep in my heart, that I am seen, I am known, and I am deeply and intimately loved. I obey because I trust him. The two are inseparable and reinforce each other in experience.

The more you trust Jesus, the easier it becomes to obey him. And as you obey Jesus, your trust is reinforced.

Yes—trust and obey. There is no other way to open your heart to tov and begin living the abundant life.

PART TWO

THE HEART OF EVERYTHING

CHAPTER 3
AWARENESS OF THE DIFFICULT

"The Christian ideal has not been tried and found wanting. It has been found difficult; and left untried."

G. K. CHESTERTON,
WHAT'S WRONG WITH THE WORLD

IT DOESN'T DEPEND ON YOU

The north wind, it blows so cold
When your back is to the son
And your dreams all turn to nightmares
When you're on the run
You lose sight of your vision
So in desperation you go for your guns
Only to find the bad guy is you
Only to find you lost the duel
– Ray Schmidt, "The Duel"

TOV MARKER

Everything in our lives – home, work, church – screams that it is up to us. But that is a lie. God is clear that we are to trust in him and depend on him alone. Learning to lean fully on him is essential to experiencing tov and living abundantly.

I thought I was doing what I was supposed to do. I did what all young men of my generation in the suburbs did: I adulted.

I went to school. Got a job. Married. Had children. Changed jobs a few times. Before I knew it and without realizing it, everything in my life quickly depended on me.

You know the feeling. Suddenly your wife, your mortgage, your bills, your job, your lifestyle, your kids' sports, your American dream all depend on you. And then you hit a speed bump or two, maybe three, and things change. Life falls apart.

Bump at work. Where your primary identity has become grounded. Bump at home. With the kids, your marriage, or both. Bump with your friends. Who has time for deep, meaningful friendships? You see them at the kids' sports games or at church, or you smile and wave as you drop the kids off at school. A quick hello and you're off to the next task on the list.

"Just smile and wave boys, just smile and wave."
– Lead Penguin, *Madagascar*[27]

The bumps create disruption. The small ones you barely notice, but inside, they disrupt you, nonetheless. And, like a 5.0 seismic tremor, you learn to manage them. Cover them over and move on.

The larger ones you roll with and work hard to keep the cargo in your life intact. But suddenly there are several together. Your boss calls you into his office on a Friday afternoon to tell you your services are no longer required. Or dishes are getting smashed, fists are hitting walls, and there is talk of divorce. Hopes, dreams, hearts, and lives are turned upside down, and there seems to be nothing you can do about it. One unintended, jumbled word leads to another, which leads to an argument. Too many careless words spill out as self-protection kicks in, and then...there's silence.

Not the silence of a peaceful, snowy afternoon in the park. Not the silence of stillness that is indicative of knowing God and tov. But the silence of anger, frustration, and fear. The silence that means one more word could bring you to the point of no return.

Everything is falling apart faster than you can put it back together. Work, if you still have a job, is insanely time-consuming. But it might be the one place you find a little "peace and quiet." If you don't have a job, OUCH! You just took a huge hit to your heart. Especially if you haven't been able to find a new one in two weeks, two months, or two years!

Your wife ends up going back to work or becomes the primary "breadwinner." Both of which confirm you're a loser. Because no matter what anyone tells you to the contrary in today's modern world, in your heart, it's your job to have a job. That is what you were made for, right? That is where the world has taught you that your real identity lies. Even if you know in your head it's not true, "loser" is screaming in your soul. Whenever someone asks you how the job search is coming. Or when you lie in bed at night wondering how in the world you got to this place.

Futility and failure in our endeavors. Like you, I never gave it much thought, but for those of us who grew up Christians, it's right there in black and white. We were warned.

> *Cursed is the ground because of you; through painful toil you will eat food from it all the days of your life. It will produce thorns and thistles for you, and you will eat the plants of the field. By the sweat of your brow you will eat your food until you return to the ground, since from it you were taken; for dust you are and to dust you will return.* – Genesis 3:17-19

That's our lot? I must have slept through that Sunday School lesson. But I know this story is true because I have lived it. And having lived it, I can honestly tell you...it doesn't depend on you because, if you're like me, you're your own worst enemy.

Nowhere in Scripture are we told that everything depends on us. There are no verses that say, "Suck it up and make it happen, because that's your job."

Quite the contrary. In Scripture, we are clearly and specifically told who we are to depend on.

> "For I am the Lord your God who takes hold of your right hand and says to you, Do not fear; I will help you." – Isaiah 41:13

> "Trust in the Lord with all your heart and lean not on your own understanding; in all your ways submit to him, and he will make your paths straight." – Proverbs 3:5-6

> "I lift up my eyes to the mountains—where does my help come from? My help comes from the Lord, the Maker of heaven and earth." – Psalm 121:1-2

> "Those who live according to the flesh have their minds set on what the flesh desires; but those who live in accordance with the Spirit have their minds set on what the Spirit desires." – Romans 8:5

> "Every good gift and every perfect gift is from above, coming down from the Father of lights, with whom there is no variation or shadow due to change." – James 1:17 ESV

Dependence is the result of trust. If we trust, we can depend upon who or what we trust.

But why is it that we separate the concepts of trust and dependence in our minds? It seems we always have a "but."

"I trust you Jesus, but..."

We live most of our lives as "either/or" creatures when we are told to be "and" people.

> *"Remain in me, as I also remain in you. No branch can bear fruit by itself; it must remain in the vine. Neither can you bear fruit unless you remain in me."* – John 15:4

Notice that it's a given that Jesus remains in you. Jesus warns us to remain in him. How? As he remains in us.

> *"Every good gift and every perfect gift is from above, coming down from the Father of lights, with whom there is no variation or shadow due to change."* – James 1:17 ESV

No variation, no shadow of turning away. Solid, fixed, secure. The Father and you. Jesus and you. Holy Spirit and you. The Father, you, and others. Jesus, you, and others. Holy Spirit, you and others.

> *"No branch can bear fruit by itself;*
> *it must remain in the vine."*

You are not the center of your universe. It is the "but" of self-reliance that so often derails the trust and dependence needed to live the abundant life we seek.

Learning to trust God—Father, Jesus, Holy Spirit—leaning fully on him in every situation is not easy to do.

Everything you have learned from the world and those around you cautions you against it. But, regardless of what your experience to the contrary is, if you really want more, if you really want to experience tov and take hold of abundant life, there is no other way. It is crucial that you realize and accept that everything doesn't depend on you.

FIGHTING THE PROCESS

"If you love me, keep my commands. And I will ask the Father, and he will give you another advocate [counselor] to help you and be with you forever—the Spirit of truth." – John 14:15-17a

TOV MARKER

We live in a culture of the immediate. Expecting everything, including change in our hearts and lives to be quick and easy ... "one and done." But the journey through tov and into abundant life requires us to accept and embrace process. A process that takes time and is at least challenging and often hard and uncomfortable. A process that, if you will follow Jesus into it, will break down the walls you put up around your heart. Setting you free to flourish for yourself and others.

Jesus told us he was sending us to counseling. And, oh, this counseling, it's going to take a while... well...actually forever.[28] Yes, you heard me right. Forever. As in never ending.

Walking with God is process. And the goal you ask for, the outcome you seek, and the purpose on whose door you knock are found in the process of going all in with God.

If we're honest, most of us don't like process, at least not in our spiritual life. We may embrace some process in our work; there are steps we take to accomplish tasks that lead to a desired outcome. But in regard to our spiritual life, we don't usually think in terms of process. Or if we do, it is a very simplified process. Something like...say the "believer's prayer," get baptized, read the Bible, go to church, and go to heaven when we die. A simple process that requires little of us.

Living in the west today, we are saturated with a culture of the immediate. We want the vast majority of things in our lives quickly. As close to "now" as we can get. That is one of the reasons so many gym memberships go unused after January thirty-first and fast food dominates most diets.

Don't tell me how to improve my health over time; just give me a pill to ... (fill in the blank). Make me stronger, help me lose weight, or relieve my pain.

Don't ask me to spend weeks, months, or maybe years working to repair the broken relationships in my life. Can't I just say, "I'm sorry" and move on?

Now that I've said the "believer's prayer" and been baptized, can't Jesus just "fix" me so I don't experience or cause others pain?

As men, we are really good at hiding. Remember Adam in the Garden? We hide by ignoring and stuffing the pain and trauma of our lives as deep as we can until we forget about it. At least we think we forget. Unfortunately, stuffing our pain is like trying to cork a volcano. Eventually, it's going to blow. Somewhere.

Even when we get a little breakthrough, we rush ahead, believing the process is done, and move on with life. At least until a deeper related issue is revealed, and we wonder why it's rearing its ugly head again. "*I thought that was healed!*" Remember, clarity is not healing. Just because we know something in our head doesn't mean it has been healed in our heart.

You probably know exactly what I mean. We especially dislike process in our life with God because it's uncharted territory. No one warned us about the time and commitment it takes for healing to occur and redemption to take hold. The time it takes for our head and our heart to align. The time it takes to experience union with God.

For food, we drive-thru or microwave. For health, there are pills or elective surgery. For entertainment, there is Instagram, TikTok, and every flavor of streaming service imaginable. For escape, there are "convenience" and liquor stores, the local "illicit pharmaceutical" salesperson, video games, and sports. For relationship, there is Facebook and text emojis.

Be honest, when was the last time you wrote a real letter? In your own hand, to someone you really care about, much less to a friend or distant relative? You know, the snail mail process of sharing what's happening in your life with someone. Think about it. Writing a letter with pen and paper. Sealing it in an envelope. Adding the delivery and return addresses. Stamping the envelope and either putting it in a mailbox or handing it to someone at the post office. If you're young enough, you quite literally may have never done it. And it takes time, thought, and intentionality.

As I said earlier, we live in a culture of the immediate, and the immediate hates process. But God—Father, Jesus, Holy Spirit—lives, moves, and has his being in process. Like any relationship, experiencing him takes time. Coming to truly love him takes time. Healing your wounds, redeeming your sin, and letting God renew your heart all take time. Even simply knowing *about* him takes time. And it is in time that we experience and participate in the process that leads to the tov heart and abundant life.

But, while time is our nemesis when it comes to process, the biggest problem most of us have with process is that process requires us to change. If we're honest, we just don't like change. So, we look for ways to get around it.

We pretend that clarity is actual healing, and that knowledge equates to experience. Neither of those are true, even if our current culture of "Knowledge as King" tells us they are. The truth is that if you try to skip the process, the outcome is uncertain and will be quite different from what you intended. For, as Yvon Chouinard says about shortcutting process, *"... if you compromise the process, you're an asshole when you start out and an asshole when you get back."*

There are no shortcuts to the tov heart and the abundant life. There is no "easy way." It takes time. And healing at the surface opens us up to the deeper work of Christ in our lives. The process takes effort and commitment, but not effort and commitment the world's way.

"For my yoke is easy and my burden is light."
– Jesus of Nazareth, Matthew 11:30

In 2007, I crashed and burned my career. The successful career of a senior executive in a prestigious non-profit corporation. To be honest, even with all my success, I was just a scared child running a mighty kingdom. The result was that I was out of work for two years. When I finally got a job, it wasn't what I thought I deserved. I believed my own press releases and thought I deserved more, bigger, better. Looking back, I was exactly where God wanted me. But at the time, I fought it tooth and nail.

For the next two years, I searched for a job that was "worthy" of me. Interview after interview, rejection after rejection. As often occurs in our lives as men, it was my wife who had to speak truth into my life.

As I was struggling with the rejections, one day she said, *"Maybe this is where God wants you for now. Stop fighting him and see what he does."*

At first it made me a little mad and I resisted her counsel but, eventually, after trying everything else, I did. I stopped fighting, and as I leaned into God and the provision he had made in my life, I found peace. To be honest, it wasn't what I wanted or where I wanted to be. But it was the place I needed to be to begin to release my pride, arrogance, and self. I had to stop fighting God to engage the process he intended to create in me the tov heart.[29]

In the end, I was in that process for thirteen years. A process that led me through different roles and diverse experiences. Professionally, personally, and spiritually. The process of growth, healing, and experiencing more of God and his provision. Thirteen years! I guess some of us learn slower than others.

As men, we all live some version of the story grounded in Genesis 3. If we are honest with ourselves, we are living out our days somewhere between death and tov. Leaning much closer to death.

In contrast to what we present to the world, many of us have gotten sidetracked, lost, distracted, or confused. How could God be so unjust? That whole Genesis 3 thing—that was Adam's fault, right? Not mine. The whole failure and futility thing. The "work till you drop" method of obedience. Punishment out to a thousand generations and all that. Seems a bit barbaric, doesn't it?

I deserve better. I'm a pretty good guy all in all. Right?

I was in this place, though I would never have put those words to it.

Even when things started to improve, it wasn't what I expected or thought I deserved. I was stuck. Stuck in "God, why are you doing this to me?" mode. Fighting him at every turn. Wanting and expecting more. Confused and disappointed that "better" wasn't happening fast enough. If it was happening at all. Often finding myself, as John Eldredge puts it, "alert and oriented times zero."[30] Clueless and frustrated.

Yes, I'm stuck in the middle with you
And I'm wondering what it is I should do
It's so hard to keep this smile from my face

AWARENESS OF THE DIFFICULT

Losing control, yeah, I'm all over the place
Clowns to the left of me
Jokers to the right
Here I am stuck in the middle with you
– Stealers Wheel, "Stuck in the Middle with You"

I am ashamed how long I was there. I was a Christian living in a prison of my own making. I couldn't see through the walls I had built around my heart with my own hands.

Yes, Jesus did say "easy and light." But, for me, my experience of the process was painful and disruptive. Why? Because I fought it tooth and nail. I had been steeped in the soup of a self-centered life since I was a boy. And, I had constructed a well-built fortress, of what I thought was protection, around my heart.

If you're like me, the process of finding freedom can be frustrating and challenging. Not because it is, but because I made it that way.

If you will accept and embrace the process Jesus initiates to create the tov heart within you. You will find freedom. Freedom to flourish. For yourself and for others. Freedom to walk the path of abundant life.

It is for freedom that Christ set us free. – Galatians 5:1

THE TOV HEART

YOUR GREATEST NEED

"We can't dabble in God and live mostly in love with the world. As the Scottish pastor and poet George MacDonald wrote, 'Man finds it hard to get what he wants, because he does not want the best; God finds it hard to give, because He would give the best, and man will not take it.' What Jesus wants to give above all else is himself, if we would choose him above all else." – John Eldredge, 30 Days to Resilient program in the Pause app

TOV MARKER

Your greatest need is not a great podcast, an insightful blog post, or the next self-help best seller. Your greatest need is God himself – Father, Jesus, Holy Spirit. The challenges you experience in life are not punishment but discipline. The discipline God uses to turn you toward himself and, if you will turn, into never ending union – oneness – with him.[31]

When we read the story of God's response to the Fall in Genesis 3:17-19, we tend to get a bit arrogant and put ourselves in God's place. We read the words with *our* voices, *our* intent, *our* judgment, *our* reproach. *"I mean, really, Adam?!?! I gave you one thing NOT to do, and you blew it!"*

But that is not how God views it. He is not punishing; he is disciplining, and those are two very different things.

Punishment has a short-term goal: to produce immediate

corrective action. In most cases, it's meant to stop undesired behavior.

Discipline, on the other hand, has a long-term goal. To create beneficial, consistent, steadfast results over time. It is, as Eugene Peterson and others have put it, "a long obedience in the same direction."

Unfortunately, in most cases, the beneficial part goes initially unseen. Because, well, discipline is process-oriented and painful. As we have seen, we don't like process, and, of course, we avoid pain at all costs.

First, like Adam, we question God's intent, thinking God is like us: full of self and muddled intent. Second, because we *are* full of self and muddled intent. We only see the immediate inconvenience, discomfort, and pain.

Yet, unlike the way we react to those around us to correct undesired behavior, God looks beyond our behavior to our need.

He knows that the action itself is of no real consequence in eternity. What is important is the motivation behind the action. In Eden, God knew that punishment would not solve Adam's and Eve's dilemma. They used their free will to become distracted and turn their eyes, ears, and hearts away from him. Jesus, quoting Isaiah in Matthew, lays it out succinctly:

> *"For this people's heart has grown dull, and with their ears they can barely hear, and their eyes they have closed, lest they should see with their eyes and hear with their ears and understand with their heart and turn, and I would heal them."*
> – Matthew 13:15 ESV

God has experienced this "turning away" in every human being since Adam and Eve. And as men, each of us has, at some point in our lives, experienced some form of the same discipline described in Genesis 3. Futility and failure in our work.

But why? Why discipline? And what is the benefit behind the discipline? God disciplined Adam and Eve because he knew their true need. They did not need to be better people. What they desperately needed was God himself.

And so, God used work and relationship. The two things core to his creation of them as man and woman, as roadblocks so that they might turn their hearts back to him for the answers to their questions.

God knows the same is true for you. Above all else you do not need to be more disciplined, find another app, or listen to another podcast. And certainly, you don't need to read another book, as good as those things may be. God knows that above all else, you need him. If you didn't know it before, you know it now. It is impossible to receive the tov heart and experience life to the full, abundant life, without union with God.

Having said this, it is my hope that you will continue reading. While this book may not be what you need above all else, I have "been there, done that" a lot. I have made mistakes and found ancient ways. What I have written in these pages is a guide, a map if you will, to help you on your journey to find union with God—Father, Jesus, Holy Spirit. And through that union and the tov heart, the abundant life Jesus promised.

I am still on this journey with you, but the map I am using is this one. Let's find abundant life together.

One more thing I want to reinforce is that abundant life is not a destination like Cancun or Paris. Abundant life is a way of living day by day, moment by moment. Abundant life is not a place you get to but an experience of life with God. Because what you really need above all else is him.

CHAPTER 4
FINDING YOUR WAY

"Should have listened to all the things I was told
But I was young and too proud at the time
Now I look at myself to find
I learn the hard way ev'ry time"

JIM CROCE,
"THE HARD WAY EVERY TIME"

MAPS

"Without geography, you're nowhere!" – Jimmy Buffett[32]

TOV MARKER

Maps are helpful. Whether digital or hardcopy they can only get you so far. It is then when, as a man, you have to make the choice to either ask someone or try to figure it out yourself. Unfortunately, for most of us, we will choose the hard way every time.

Mobile map applications are pretty cool and mostly helpful. I say "mostly" because there are those times when your map app tells you to make a left turn into a rock quarry or a swamp as you're trying to find your way to the nearest coffee shop.

In the olden days, maps were paper—hardcopy. A single, huge sheet of paper folded to fit into your glove compartment but could never quite get folded back the same way twice. Or, for more urban locations, a ten by fourteen-inch spiral bound book for a particular regional or city area.

When I learned to drive, if you didn't know how to get where you wanted to go, you only had three options. Option 1: Ask someone and have them tell you how to get there, hoping they really knew the way. Option 2: Get a paper map and plot the course to follow. Option 3: Just start driving and figure it out as you went along. Hopefully getting to your destination at some point.

I usually chose Option 2 or Option 3 since they didn't involve confessing to another person that I didn't know where I was going. Confessing weakness to a friend, much less to a total stranger, is just not a guy thing. And weakness includes not knowing where you are going.

Whenever I had a date planned, a day or two before, I would pull out the map book and figure out how to get to my date's house. Then I would drive the route. That way, when date night rolled around, I didn't look like an idiot trying to find my way. Some may call it stalking, but for me, it was self-preservation. In the suburban area where I lived, those map books became a lifeline for my dating life.

The only time I would break down and use Option 1 was in the direst emergency. After Option 2 had failed and time didn't allow for the meandering that typically accompanied Option 3.

Left to determine my own path, I would usually choose the hard way every time. Not because it was hard but because it was the best way to self-protect. And self-protection was more important than efficiency.

LOST ON THE WAY

"If I start outsourcing all my navigation to a little talking box in my car, I'm sort of screwed. I'm going to lose my car in the parking lot every single time." – Ken Jennings[33]

TOV MARKER

It's hard to admit we need help navigating life. So, we lie to the world. We pose. We present to the world a man who has it all together, when in truth we don't. It's a lie that creates tension and robs us of the ability to truly live. To find the tov heart and the way to abundant life, you must release the tension by stepping into truth.

Navigating life is pretty much the same deal. We kind of know where we want to go, but we're too embarrassed to ask for directions. As a result, we get lost in the parking lot of our day-to-day lives. That results in our leaning more and more into ourselves to just "man up" and figure it out. Call it pride or arrogance, the result is the same.

At some point many of us become orphans, whether by force or preference, and we end up lost, wandering around a lot.

We buy some self-help book recommended by one of our friends. We listen to podcasts or watch a YouTube video, and we just figure it out. Whatever "it" is. Repairing your car, rewiring an electrical outlet, unclogging a drain, restoring a relationship, building a shed, starting a fire, sharpening a knife, smoking a cigar, or walking with God. The list is long and diverse. The Internet and its associated mobile apps have actually made it easier to live as an orphan. Who needs to go to friends or family for advice when you have YouTube and Google? They're available twenty-four seven, even in the darkest hours of the night, right?

The longer I live, the more I realize the extent of what I was never taught and just don't know. And here's my confession. Google and YouTube are my usual go-tos. Because I don't have anyone in my life who has "been there, done that" for most things. And, even if I do in some areas, they're usually not men I can trust with my vulnerability. But to be completely honest, I have a few trustworthy men in my life. But they are a precious few.

Now, I realize some of you do have men in your lives to provide you with guidance and encouragement. What we used to call apprenticeship. If you do, you are blessed beyond measure. But I can be pretty sure that even then, there are places where you hold back. Places it's hard to share even with Jesus.

It goes back to pride and arrogance, but it's much deeper than that. The usual motivation behind pride and arrogance is fear. Fear of being really seen and known. Seen and known not as strong and capable, but as unsure and questioning. As John Eldredge says in his book *Wild at Heart*, a man's primary question in life is "*Do I have what it takes?*"[34] Much of the time the answer to that question is "No."

When I was in my early teens, I was blessed to spend four summers on my grandmother's farm. My grandfather had died when I was young and my grandmother lived in the family home with one of her sons, my uncle Curt, and his wife, Aunt Grey. I got some of my basic life questions answered on that farm during those years. Among a host of other things, I learned how to milk cows. Cut, rake, and bail hay. Gather chicken eggs, care for a vegetable garden, and drive a tractor, truck, and car. I learned that, under the category of "doing things," I did have what it takes. I had the ability to do things, figure stuff out, and get things done. It was a God-given ability to succeed in the world. But my ability to get physical things done in the world allowed me to put a facade of capability over the less visible areas of my life. If you're capable in areas that can be seen, you're capable in the areas that cannot, right? It was a facade that, for many years, locked up my heart and prevented me from being present to both myself and others. And...I learned to lie.

One day I was chopping wood in the corn crib and accidentally cut a slice of skin back on the knuckle of my left thumb. It was a pretty good whack accompanied by a substantial flow of blood. I ran to the house and told Aunt Grey that I was running through the corn crib and tripped and fell hitting my thumb on the double-headed axe that was nearby. I'm not sure if she believed me, but she never questioned me any deeper. At the time, I couldn't have told you why I changed the story. But looking back, the reason is all too clear. As a fatherless boy, an orphan of my own making, I didn't want her to know my vulnerability. I didn't want her or anyone else to know that I didn't have what it takes. I still have the scar of that accident on both my thumb and my heart.

As a result, I quickly stepped into my primary mode of self-protection ... deception. A small lie that led to more lies that all stemmed from the core fear that I didn't really have what it takes. I wasn't good enough.

Throughout my life, my facade of being everything to everyone has manifested itself in a core set of lies. Not confronting fear led to an inability to connect with others deeply. Which has been my greatest weakness and the source of my greatest failures. I either lied to make sure my reputation for capability remained intact or, and this was the deadliest, I ran away.

I was afraid and I was a coward. I avoided conflict with a passion.

All of us have felt the assault of the world at some point, whether from family, friends, or colleagues. And all of us have built some kind of protective wall around our hearts to deflect the fear, pain, or trauma that comes from life. A wall that tells the world that we have what it takes when in fact the truth is just the opposite. The external personification of capability. The poser.

Others have coined and used the term. I use it here to put a name to what is true of us all. Whether it's smaller poses that protect the vulnerable places in our hearts or a large pose that defines the man we present to the world, we all pose. You know it's true.

The poser is your shield when the arrows fly. He is your go-to when someone purposely or accidentally steps on a wounded place in your heart. Those places that may have scabbed over, but, like Frodo's wound from the Morgul blade, never truly healed. So, while the poser protects us from having our weaknesses exposed, he also creates a core disassociation with reality. A lie. A lie that both blinds and binds us. A lie that leads to more lies. A lie the Evil One then uses to separate us from God and from others.

Standing alongside our core question of "Do I have what it takes?" resides every man's core desire. To be known and loved for who he truly is. Not the poser, but the man. It's a cognitive dissonance that keeps us on edge and lost.

Like an uncontrolled diabetic who desperately wants to eat a dozen jelly donuts. He also knows the next bite might kill him. The result is a tension that robs us of peace, joy, and love. Tension that ensures we will not be seen, known, and loved for the man we truly are, even though it is what our heart desperately desires.

If we want to find the tov heart and the way to abundant life, we must release this tension. But the only way to release the tension is to trust Jesus and boldly step into truth.

> *"To the Jews who had believed him, Jesus said, "If you hold to my teaching, you are really my disciples. Then you will know the truth, and the truth will set you free." – John 8:31-32*

PATH TO FREEDOM

"The Spirit of the Lord is on me,
  because he has anointed me
  to proclaim good news to the poor.
He has sent me to proclaim freedom for the prisoners
  and recovery of sight for the blind,
to set the oppressed free,
  to proclaim the year of the Lord's favor."
– Jesus of Nazareth, Luke 4:18-19

TOV MARKER

As truth moves from your head to your heart, the re-creation of the tov heart within you begins.

I had failed miserably financially, and my wife didn't know how bad it was. We were getting to the end of our resources, and one night as I was getting ready for bed, Jesus said, *You need to tell her.* I replied, *I can't. She'll leave me and I will lose the kids. Everything.*

He softly repeated, *You need to tell her. I can't,* I replied. At that point, Jesus asked me one of the two most important questions of my life. *Do you trust me?* I told him, *Yes, Lord, but I don't know how to tell her.* Like the cripple at Bethesda, I didn't really answer his question. I gave him an excuse. He softly asked me again. *Do you trust me?* I said, *Yes, I do, Lord, but I don't know how. You'll have to help me.* That's how I fell asleep.

The next morning, the first thing I did when I woke up was tell her.

I don't know how that worked—more on that later—but the important thing right now is that I stepped into the truth.

To be clear, it wasn't all roses and lollypops from that point forward. Not in any way.

I had betrayed trust. And because we as human beings cannot see the motivations and movements of the heart; it has been a long hard road to regain her trust. It has been the longest, hardest journey of my life. But the day I told her, I released the tension, and I stepped into truth not knowing the outcome.

Jesus led me to the place where I knew the truth, acted on the truth, and the truth set me free. "Free" not in the sense of a lack of turmoil and pain, but free in my heart through truth.

A large part of the poser was defeated that day. Part of the wall around my heart was knocked down. I was finally known for who I truly was. And though it was pretty ugly and massively painful for my family, I was set free.

That morning was also the beginning of the defeat of fear in my life. The exhortations of Scripture began to move silently from my head to my heart.

"Cast all your anxiety on him because he cares for you."
– 1 Peter 5:7

"So do not fear, for I am with you; do not be dismayed, for I am your God. I will strengthen you and help you; I will uphold you with my righteous right hand." – Isaiah 41:10

"Peace I leave with you; my peace I give you. I do not give to you as the world gives. Do not let your hearts be troubled and do not be afraid." – John 14:27

As truth moves from your head to your heart, the re-creation of the tov heart begins. The poser and all the self-protection built up within you begins to be broken down and disarmed.

Your self-protection may not show up as fear. It may manifest itself in anger, frustration, or rage. It may show up as always being "right," dismissal, blame shifting, or any of the million ways we have found to live life separated from truth. Ways we try to control our image and our destiny. But it is only in and through truth that you are really set free.

"... know the truth, and the truth will set you free."

SLOW THE CLOCK DOWN

"For fast-acting relief, try slowing down." – Lily Tomlin

TOV MARKER

We are addicted to technology and the pace of life that technology dictates. Slowing down your pace provides space in you and around you for life to flourish.

When I was young, my life was full of the outdoors. Playing army in the grass, dirt clog battles with my friends, searching for crayfish in the creek behind my house, and bike rides to nowhere. When I talked to my friends, I used my voice, and we physically got together. We shared our hopes and dreams, our failures and loves, our pain and joy face to face.

For all the good that technology has brought to society, technology has become yet another drug to which we have become addicted. A wall between us and relationship.

Now, don't get me wrong. Like many, my life is dependent upon technology. My job and my ability to provide for my family, my career and "who I am as a man" have been deeply tied to technology.

Many people have and continue to make their fortunes off and through technology. But for many others, especially the youngest, most vulnerable of us, technology is just another opioid. Another distraction, another path into sedation and isolation.

No wonder mental health problems are the number one cause of disability worldwide. We live life, for the most part, only in our small stories, literally at the speed of light. Our lives are experienced primarily through technology. TikTok, X, Instagram, Facebook, YouTube, or whatever the latest social media fad is.

On top of that, we've become voyeurs of each other's small stories. Killing our ability and capability to relate with each other and the larger story we were created to actively, personally engage. We've lost the will to slow down and lean into our lives and relationships in a more relaxed, deliberate way.

By "small story" I mean the life you live with you at the center. By "larger story" I mean the story God has invited you into. The story he wants you to be an integral part of, with him the center.

This presents us with a question. Is there a way to oppose the technology fueled pace of today's world and begin living out of the tov heart? In his book about Sabbath, Wayne Muller says:

"Because we do not rest, we look our way. We miss the compass points that would show us where to go, we bypass the nourishment that would give us succor. We miss the quiet that would give us wisdom. We miss the joy and love born of effortless delight."[35]

"Be still, and know that I am God; I will be exalted among the nations, I will be exalted in the earth." The Lord Almighty is with us; the God of Jacob is our fortress." – Psalm 46:10-11

The dangers of speed are clear. We get off track and lose our way. We miss the nourishment we need to really live and the quietness that instills wisdom. We fly past the joy and love which are core to living life abundantly. The good news is that we can slow down the ticking clock. There is a way. If we will be still. If we will slow down the ticking clock.

In the 2014 sports movie *Draft Day*,[36] the protagonist, Sonny Weaver Jr., has an instructive exchange with his love interest, Alli.

Sonny: *"I'm makin' mistakes.* [Pause and deep sigh] *Remember the '89 Super Bowl?"*

Alli: *"Forty-niners-Bengals. Niners down by three, 3:20 left in the game. Ninety-three yard winning drive, Taylor beats the weak safety for a ten-yard TD."*

Sonny: *"Yeah, but before the drive. Joe Montana's in the huddle. Right? And unbelievably, somehow spots the actor John Candy in the stands. He points at him and asks the guys in the huddle, 'Hey, isn't that John Candy?' They couldn't believe the balls on him. To be that*

> calm, in that game, at that moment. His guys instantly relax; they march...um..."

Alli: "Ninety-three yards."

Sonny: "Ninety-three yards. Montana throws a little slant to Taylor. Forty-Niners win the Super Bowl."

Alli: "Great game."

Sonny: "It was a great game. No one can stop a ticking clock. But the great ones, the great ones always find a way to slow it down."

As a son of the Living God, you are one of the "great ones." You can slow down the ticking clock. You can limit and even remove the interruptions, distractions, and addictions that dull your senses. That stands between you and others. Between you and union with God.

In his Super Bowl moment, Joe Montana was living out of the tov heart, though I doubt very much he recognized it as such. He was able to create an environment for himself and his teammates where life flourished. Even if it was only for a little while.

SITUATIONAL AWARENESS

I shall be telling this with a sigh
Somewhere ages and ages hence:
Two roads diverged in a wood, and I—
I took the one less traveled by,
And that has made all the difference.
– "The Road Not Taken," Robert Frost[37]

TOV MARKER

On this journey you need to understand where the topography is steep and challenging. If there are rivers to cross, are there fords, or do you have to swim? Are there natural places to rest, or must they be created along the way? Nourishment. Water. Shelter. Weather. All must be considered and prepared for. However, as much as you try to prepare, your knowledge of the way is only as good as your map and your guide.

The movie *Free Solo*[38] documents Alex Honnold's quest to perform the first-ever free solo climb—a climb without protection—of the Freerider route on El Capitan in Yosemite National Park.

The film records Alex's planning and preparation for the most dangerous climb of his life.[39] His preparation is focused and intense with at least fifteen climbs of the same route with protection prior to his execution of the free solo.

Before setting off on any journey, it is always a good idea to look ahead. Get the lay of the land. Plan your itinerary. Understand the nuances and familiarize yourself with the terrain to come.

It is also important to remember that this journey is not "one and done." Like Honnold, you may need to go over the same ground multiple times to be able to fully step into tov and abundant life. Please understand that this doesn't mean you're blowing it or can't get it right. Diminishment is not an attribute of Jesus' work in our lives.

Think about it for a minute: How many times in your life have you really experienced a "one and done" scenario? Almost never, right? Whether it's learning to ride a bike, play the guitar, or adjusting the timing on a 1973 Datsun 240Z. It takes practice to get it right.

My teenage friends and I used a phrase when working on cars: "Do it the first time to learn, the second time to do it right." And the more complex the activity, the more time it takes to "get it right."

When it comes to tov and the abundant life, I don't believe we ever get it completely "right." At least not in this world. I say this not to discourage you but to remove some of the pressure.

As men, we always want to "get it right." Right?

God is not after "right;" he is after the healing and renewal of your heart. He is after the harvest he intended in and through you when you were created. He is after the restoration of tov within you. The tov heart.

I want you to hear me clearly here. Following God and seeking the tov heart and the abundant life is not one-size-fits-all. The exact path for your journey is singular and unique to you. Yes, we are following a map. But the map is context, not detail. The map is guidance, not formula.

For the day-to-day details of this journey, set in the context of your personal story, you also need a Master Guide.

It is impossible to know and anticipate every twist and turn of the journey. You'd feel more confident and prepared if you knew exactly how everything was going to play out. But it's just not possible. We can't even be sure of our next breath much less how tomorrow, next week, next month or next year will unfold. The only place you can live is in each moment of each day as it unfolds.

Lucky for us, we have a Master Guide who, not only has been there and done that, but also knows the way ahead. The nuances and the choices. Specific to our lives and journey. So, we must stay close. Closer than a brother.[40] And, many times we may need him to carry us. Because as American theologian and philosopher Francis Schaeffer said, in this world, we will only receive substantial or partial healing.

> *The alternatives are not between being perfect or being nothing. Just as people smash marriages because they are looking for what is romantically and sexually perfect and in this poor world do not find it, so human beings often smash what could have been possible in a true church or true Christian group. It is not just the "they" involved who are not yet perfect, but the "I" is not yet perfect either. In the absence of present perfection, Christians are to help each other on to increasingly substantial healing on the basis of the finished work of Christ. This is our calling.*[41]

If you're like me, you want as much substantial healing as you can get. More importantly, you also want it for others.

Situational awareness is crucial to every journey you take in life. You need to be aware of the road ahead. Every twist and turn, every change in elevation, every potential obstacle and obstruction. All must be considered and prepared for. Yet, as much as you try to prepare, your knowledge of the way is only as good as your map and your guide. Because, as the old saying goes, "*Shit happens.*"

This journey is no different. But instead of trekking into the wilderness of the great outdoors or going on vacation, we are on a journey to find abundant life.

The good news is that abundant life is not wishful thinking or a figment of someone's imagination. The tov heart is not a dream left over from Eden. The tov heart and abundant life exist and can be found. Not only found but experienced and lived. A way of life unperturbed by any circumstance.

But, as with most epic journeys in our lives, it will often be hard, sometimes painful, and may appear perilous. There are many things to overcome: obstacles and traps, obstructions and delays. But, brother, the result is unimaginable, and you have what it takes. The tov heart and abundant life can be yours for the living.

And guess what? Remember that Master Guide I mentioned earlier? You have one, and the good news is, it isn't me. It's Jesus.

CHAPTER 5
UNCONSIDERED ASCENTS

"So we fix our eyes not on what is seen, but on what is unseen, since what is seen is temporary, but what is unseen is eternal."

2 CORINTHIANS 4:18

THE UNSEEN

"It is not the mountain we conquer, but ourselves."
– Sir Edmund Hillary[42]

TOV MARKER
There are three ascents crucial to the journey. The "if" in scripture, the control of our will, and the allowance for mystery. They are not simply ideas to be considered. They are truths to be confronted and treasured.

There are three crucial "ascents" on our journey that go largely unconsidered today. I call them ascents because, as in climbing, each requires preparation and effort. And each varies in their level of difficulty, distance covered, and altitude.

The concept of ascents in our walk with God is not new. Psalms 120 to 134 are called the Songs of Ascent because Jews traveling to Jerusalem for one of the three primary annual Jewish festivals traditionally sang these songs on the uphill road or ascent to the city. The "Songs of Ascent" provided these pilgrims with a united source of praise, remembrance, encouragement, and worship.

The ascents I am referring to are ancient ascents known to saints who have traveled the road before us. They are not hidden. They've always been available. But they are often unseen, untried, and unacknowledged, nonetheless.

If they are glimpsed at all, we sweep by them with no more consideration and, possibly, the same annoyance given a fly or gnat buzzing around our head. They are, in the order of our consideration,

- *the "if" in Scripture*
- *control of our will*
- *the allowance for mystery*

If, Will, and Mystery.

I also call them ascents because each one requires something of us. We must exert ourselves to mine their fruit. And to benefit, we must prepare and leave something behind.

Generally, we are really good at preparation. We prepare all the time. For travel, meetings, presentations, performances, meals, and exercise. But the biggest problems we find with preparation are the obstacles we fail to prepare for. Those things that, either due to our unwillingness or blindness, are unseen and so we fail to take them into account as we prepare.

It can be hard to leave things behind. Especially, when we believe they are crucial to our identity as a man. Newton's third law of gravity states simply that if you want to get somewhere, you must leave something behind. Regarding tov and the abundant life, the something you must leave behind is you. Not the you, created in the image of God before the foundation of the world, but the you that constructed the poser. The you built over time to hide your true self from the world. What the Apostle Paul called, "your old self."

"You were taught, with regard to your former way of life, to put off your old self, which is being corrupted by its deceitful desires;

> *to be made new in the attitude of your minds; and to put on the new self, created to be like God in true righteousness and holiness."* – Ephesians 4:22-24

Morgan Snyder quotes a friend who once told him, *"The only problem with vacation is that I go with me."*

As we embark, it is important for us to name and consciously consider these crucial ascents. They are crucial to our journey because they are core ascents our hearts must take toward tov. Each ascent takes our hearts closer to God—Father, Jesus, Holy Spirit—and deeper into our tov heart.

Jesus engaged these ascents as he approached the cross.

> *"As the time approached for him to be taken up to heaven, Jesus resolutely set out for Jerusalem."* – Luke 9:51

Jesus was determined and could not and would not be turned aside from the path the Father set before him. Echoing the power of God spoken of by Isaiah:

> *"Because the Sovereign Lord helps me, I will not be disgraced. Therefore have I set my face like flint, and I know I will not be put to shame."* – Isaiah 50:7

These ascents are not optional cruise excursions. And they are not just ideas to be considered and acknowledged in our minds. If you are to embark on this journey, these ascents must be confronted and "treasured up" in your heart. If not ...

UNCONSIDERED ASCENTS

"It isn't the mountains ahead to climb that wears you out; it's the pebble in your shoe." – Muhammad Ali

Most of the time, the pebbles in our shoes go unseen and unconsidered. That is until they start tearing a hole in your foot.

THE QUESTION OF "IF"

"If you can keep your head when all about you
    Are losing theirs and blaming it on you;
If you can trust yourself when all men doubt you,
    But make allowance for their doubting too..."
– "If," Rudyard Kipling

TOV MARKER
Scripture is full of IF. Yet we most often ignore the IF to get to the "good stuff", the blessing and promises of God. We must embrace the IF and make a choice. Choose God above all else ... or not.
Tov or death.

The poem "If" hung over the dresser in my childhood bedroom until my mother sold her house in 2000. It was written by nineteenth/twentieth-century British poet and author Rudyard Kipling, most famous for his story *The Jungle Book*.

The poem "If" is a powerful declaration both over and for his son. Advice that the son must actively choose to live out to reap the benefit.

If? Then ...

*"Yours is the Earth and everything that's in it,
And—which is more—you'll be a Man, my son!"*

Our relationship with God is similar. We must actively choose to live in alignment with him for us to receive the promises of Scripture.

Early on, I had no clue who Rudyard Kipling was. There was no connection with him other than the fact that my mother had placed his poem on the wall above my dresser. The same is true when we first hear of Jesus and read his Word. There is no real connection. Nothing more than someone else's assurance that both are important.

Unfortunately, most of us first learn about Jesus and his words during times of pain, loss, or trauma. Already in a dissociative state of mind, our first response to this introduction is something religious like, "What? Oh, sure!" said in an unbelieving, condescending tone. I mean, we've been lied to most of our lives, and we've learned that it is more than prudent to be skeptical of what we're told.

Even for those of us who have grown up in the church, early on, the Bible is very much like a poem hanging on the wall above your dresser. Nice words, but what do they mean? And the author? Well, you really don't know him from Rudyard Kipling or Adam, for that matter.

Regardless of the path we take, as we come to know the author, the Bible begins to come alive and provides living water[43] that overflows from within us into the world. It is in God—Father, Jesus, and Holy Spirit—that we learn to *"live and move and have our being."*[44] It is in God that we find life, love, and refuge. *IF.*

Too often, we overlook the *IF* in Scripture. Take, for example, Psalm 91. As one of the most recognized refuge psalms in the Bible, it is both powerful and encouraging. But there is an important *IF* that, in our excitement to get to the "good" stuff, we too often run past. We ignore it at our own peril, setting ourselves up for disappointment and confusion.

> *If you say, "The Lord is my refuge,"*
> *and you make the Most High your dwelling,*
> *no harm will overtake you,*
> *no disaster will come near your tent.*
> *For he will command his angels concerning you*
> *to guard you in all your ways;*
> *they will lift you up in their hands,*
> *so that you will not strike your foot against a stone.*
> *You will tread on the lion and the cobra;*
> *you will trample the great lion and the serpent.*
> – Psalm 91:9-13

Do you see the *IF*? Why do we so easily ignore the *IF*? First, because the promises in this psalm are abundant. They comprise fifteen of the sixteen verses. The promises of God overflow Scripture just as they will overflow our lives...*IF*. Notice that the *IF* is short and sweet, but the promises are abundant and overflowing. So much so that we often rush right on by the *IF*. But the theme of Psalm 91 is a simple one: make God your refuge and home. If you do, you will be protected, no matter what happens around you.

The second reason is that we just don't like the *IF*. John Eldredge put it this way: *"The idea of 'if' is very irritating to human* nature, but it is very true to reality and true to the heart of God."⁴⁵ We want the abundance but without conditions. We just want to live our lives the way we want. We can be very stubborn creatures.

When one of my former pastors was preparing to plant his church, he visited the homes in the local community and interviewed the residents. He asked about their lives, their aspirations, and their hopes and dreams.

What did he find out? Most people wanted their current lives—just a little better. Not totally unexpected. But there is danger in taking this posture in our lives.

Jesus provides us with a stark warning,

> *"Remember what happened to Lot's wife. If you cling to your life, you will lose it, and if you let your life go, you will save it."*
> – Luke 10:32-33 NLT

The *IF* here comes with a choice: "cling to your life" or "let your life go." Lose your life or save it. The choice is binary. And, the choice has consequences. Every choice we make does. In this case, the choice can be deadly, or the choice can be bountiful and full of life—tov. Either/Or. There is no middle ground. No Switzerland.

We find a similar theme in Proverbs 3:5-6:

> *Trust in the Lord with all your heart*
>   *and lean not on your own understanding;*
> *in all your ways submit to him,*
>   *and he will make your paths straight.*

Do you see the *IF*? It's more subtle here. *IF* you trust with all your heart. *IF* you submit to God in everything. Then he will make your paths straight. If you don't, well, the words crooked, twisty, rough, and hilly come to mind.

Another example of *IF* is found in John 15, Jesus' famous "I am the vine" passage.

> *"I am the vine; you are the branches. If you remain in me and I in you, you will bear much fruit; apart from me you can do nothing."* – John 15:5

Jesus himself delivers the *IF*. You will bear much fruit … *IF*. *IF* you remain in him. Align yourself with him. Follow him. Do what he says. But if you don't, well, look at verse 6. *"If you do not remain in me, you are like a branch that is thrown away and withers; such branches are picked up, thrown into the fire and burned."*

But why, if God is good, does he not just give us the promise outright? Why only *IF*?

Because God knows that, like Adam and Eve in Eden, we need him more than we need anything else. And because of his love for us, he will not force us to seek, trust, and love him. He wants our full heart, not simply our mental assent to his existence. Our hearts are where our convictions are formed. Where we store up our treasure. And it is from our hearts that we truly live and love. So, we must choose. If we want God, if we want the promise, tov and the abundant life, we must choose the *IF*.

But let me be clear: you are not told *IF* as a form of coercion or punishment. For you to flourish and grow, to be strong and secure, and to live life fully and abundantly, above all else you need him.

Since the Fall in the Garden of Eden, God has made it clear that if we want full, abundant life, we must choose him. Aligning ourselves with his will and seeking union with him to do so as we listen to his voice. We must desire God above all else because everything we seek, and desire flows from him.

Life: The River of Life flowing from the throne of God, providing abundance.[46]

Love: The Love of God as a shield and hedge of protection. Strength, joy, and hope against fear and confusion. More abundance.[47]

Healing and Renewal: The Creation Glory of God that made all that is. As originally designed and intended and works today to restore what has been lost. More abundance still.[48]

The Life, Love, and Glory of God in, over, and through you; bursting forth into more life, more love, and more glory. The glory God intended to release upon the world when he created you. A harvest thirty, sixty, a hundred times what was sown.[49] But only *IF* you choose God above all else.

Above your pain and your ease. Above your sorrow and your joy. Above your fear and your love. Above your shame and your success. Above your guilt and your forgiveness. Everything you desire, love, and hope for flows from your union with God.

IF.

WILL YOU?

"Our Father in heaven, hallowed be your name, your kingdom come, your will be done, on earth as it is in heaven..." – Matthew 6:9-10

TOV MARKER
Your will directs every decision of your life. Most of the time it is on autopilot, engaged with little or no conscious thought. But your choices matter. They matter a lot. When we become hurt, weary, or bored we tend to go to our addictions. They are a known, easy path and, at least for a little while, we seem to find comfort there. Never mind the hangover. The resulting guilt, shame, or frustration. Jesus told us to exercise our will on purpose and come to him for comfort instead. It is that easy. And that hard.

Your will is an interesting thing. Actually, it is much more than interesting. Your will, whether you realize it or not, directs every decision of your life.

Jesus was engaging the man's will when he asked the cripple at the Bethesda pool the simple question. *"Do you want to get well?"*[50] The cripple had been in his current circumstances so long he had forgotten what he really wanted. He suppressed his own will. In answering Jesus, he completely ignored Jesus' question and went into a dissertation on why he couldn't get to the pool to be healed.

Jesus approached the same question from a different direction when he spoke with the blind man.[51] When the blind man approached him, Jesus asked, *"What do you want me to do for you?"*

As people created in the image of God, our will is a very powerful thing, because God's will is.

> *"You are worthy, our Lord and God, to receive glory and honor and power, for you created all things, and by your will they were created and have their being."* – Revelation 4:11

> *"In the beginning was the Word, and the Word was with God, and the Word was God. He was with God in the beginning. Through him all things were made; without him nothing was made that has been made."* – John 1:1-3

Jesus created everything by and through his will. Jesus taught his disciples and us to pray that the Father's will would be done here on earth as it is in heaven[52] because God's will makes things happen. And whether we admit it or not, whether we like it or not, our will also makes things happen—good and bad.

Within the limited domain of the small kingdom that is your life, you make things happen by and through your will. This is what Blaise Pascal called *"the dignity of causality."*[53] Every person is invested with this capability as part of being *"fearfully and wonderfully made."*[54]

As the king of the kingdom that is your life, you have control there. Maybe not over everything that happens to you, but definitely in how you react and respond. The decisions you make, and the actions you take.

If we really think about it, our will scares us. We don't like the fact that we have that much power and control. And we mostly try to shy away from the responsibility this implies. Like the crippled man at Bethesda, we need to be encouraged to use our will. Or like the blind man along the road, we need to be prodded. Because it is not often that we consciously engage our will.

Subconsciously, however, your will is always at work. From the moment you wake up until you fall asleep, your will is actively present and engaged. From the routine to the impactful, you use your will moment by moment, day in and day out. From choosing the clothes you wear or the food you eat. To whether to lean into your addiction of choice when tired, oppressed, or bored. Your will is constantly engaged.

Most of the time, we don't give our will much thought. Bill Watterson, the creator of Calvin and Hobbes, put it this way:

> "I'm killing time while I wait for life to shower me with meaning and happiness."

There's the problem. For the most part, we are coasters. We live each day not on purpose, but by accident. Not as kings and queens of a kingdom. But as slaves to the temptations of the world, the deception of the Evil One, and our own ease and comfort.

I will admit that most decisions we make each day are relatively benign. But when was the last time you spent hours upon hours playing video games? Scrolling through Instagram reels? Staying late at the office to avoid conflict or boredom at home? Masturbating to pornography? Getting lost in the bar down the street or a six-pack in your refrigerator? Or sports ... what about sports? And just because I haven't mentioned your particular addiction doesn't mean it doesn't exist or matter.

You know what your addiction of choice is. Whatever you go to for comfort, peace, or support, other than God, when you are hurt, weary, or bored. Some of our addictions are "big" ones. But there are a multitude of "little" choices we make, apart from God, that kill our heart. The wellspring of life.[55] Unfortunately, there is often a hangover. Shame, guilt, or frustration are usually the residue of going to our comforters. And comfort is not what our hearts really need; rest.

Jesus said, "*Come to me, all you who are weary and burdened, and I will give you rest.*"[56]

Over the course of my life, I have exercised my will millions, perhaps billions of times. I have chosen both well and poorly. I have chosen Jesus, and I have not. Too many times, I have gone to other "comforters" by default rather than to Jesus on purpose.

It is impossible to coast to Jesus. To "come to him," you must act on purpose. You must consciously exercise your will. You must decide and choose to do it. It is as simple and as hard as that.

The only real question is, "*Will you?*"

MYSTERY AS A WAY OF LIFE

"... reality is far more extensive than our habitual perception of it."
– Eugene Peterson, *Run with the Horses*[57]

"The fact that we have reduced the sacred mystery of the Church to a one-hour service we attend is staggering."
– Francis Chan, *Letters to the Church*[58]

TOV MARKER

Mystery is something most of us don't consider outside of the context of something we must figure out. However, we live in two worlds at the same time. The physical and the spiritual. The physical is the world around us and generally viewed as something we can figure out in our head. The spiritual is full of true mystery that is primarily experienced in our heart. You don't have to understand the mystery of God's movement in your life to experience its benefit. But you must choose to trust the mystery of God at work in your life and the life of others. Even if you don't understand how it works.

What do you think of when you hear the word "mystery"? For most of us, a mystery is something to be figured out. A problem to be solved, or a question to be definitively answered.

But often with God, it's exactly the opposite.

One Sunday morning I headed to church early. I was Greeting Team lead and needed to be there early to make sure everything was set up and ready to go. This Sunday was the Sunday before Veteran's Day. Veteran's Sunday.

As I was blasting down the highway, only slightly exceeding the speed limit, I saw a man ahead of me walking along the side of the road. He was dressed in fatigues and was carrying a large military duffle on his back.

I immediately thought to myself, *Stop and ask him if he'd like to come to church.* My next thought was one of concern, *What if I bring him and he acts up?* These two conflicting thoughts came quickly. Within a second of each other as I approached him at 60 miles per hour.

As I drove past him, I clearly heard Jesus ask me one of the two most important questions of my life.

"*Is your fear greater than my love?*"

Immediately I turned around and stopped to pick him up.

How did Jesus do that? He spoke directly to my mind and heart at the same time. With clarity and insight regarding the deepest issue of my life. Fear. I don't have a clue regarding the mechanism of what occurred, but I heard Jesus speak.

From that point on, God put an exclamation point on the reality of mystery being part and parcel of my walk with him. I don't have to know how "it" works to benefit from or enjoy the experience of God's work in my life and the lives of others.

In our quest for the tov heart and the abundant life, remember that we are dealing with the God of the universe.

> *"For my thoughts are not your thoughts,*
> *neither are your ways my ways, declares the Lord.*
> *As the heavens are higher than the earth,*
> *so are my ways higher than your ways*
> *and my thoughts than your thoughts."*
> – Isaiah 55:8-9

It's also important to remember that God is not linear. We are. We can only do one thing at a time. He can do everything at once. Heal, redeem, restore, create, speak, and act. And he performs each perfectly and easily, with no loss of focus or attention.

We like to think we can "multi-task," do many things at once, but that's just an illusion. What we really do is time-slice. One thing at a time, imperfectly and haltingly.

Though we may shift from one thing to another rapidly, it is still one thing at a time. And the faster we time-slice, the less focused we become.

How does God do it? Mystery. It's unknown and not possible to know in the sense that one plus one equals two. While God's work in our lives provides for an amazing amount of knowledge. His deepest, most important work is in the heart.

In our heads we comprehend what we can figure out. Understand in our three-dimensional world. But it is in our hearts that we can grasp the truth of the mystery of God's work in and through our lives. Even if we don't understand it in our minds. This is what the Apostle Paul calls trust.[59] His secret of being content in every circumstance.[60]

You don't have to understand something in your head to know and experience it in your heart.

Take a kiss for instance. A passionate kiss is something you experience not in your head but in your heart. Your heart knows the depth of the experience. Without your head understanding the physiology or biology.

Anger is an emotion we often feel. We understand the circumstances of our anger. But we don't comprehend the biophysical forces that move our hearts throughout the stages of anger. From agitation to hatred and everything in between.

Let's take a few minutes to do an exercise. Picture your favorite place on earth. Rest in the experience of it.

Now ask yourself, why is it your favorite? What do you feel when you go there? Why does it make you feel that way?

My guess is that just asking those questions does damage the experience of the place. Doesn't the most joy, peace, and enjoyment occur when you simply experience something without the analysis?

Because we are created in the image of God, we can experience things in their true multi-faceted existence. But to do this requires us to embrace mystery. To know without knowing.

Recently Jesus gave me a bit of rescue in the phrase *"Trust Without Understanding."* It surprised me. To be honest, it shocked me a bit. But it's right there in the Bible. Solomon tells us in one of his most famous proverbs.

> *"Trust in the Lord with all your heart and lean not on your own understanding; in all your ways acknowledge him, and he will make your paths straight."* – Proverbs 3:5-6 NIV 1984

Trust without understanding.

Like most of us, I have grown up in a world of reason and understanding, science and proof. Mental assent is the arbiter of truth. That's how most of us live day to day: bound by our own understanding.

Yet I have come to realize that most of the fear in my life has been driven by the limits of my own understanding. Fear of losing my job. Fear of illness. Fear about the economy. Fear of political outcome. Fear of...fill in the blank.

I am mortal. Finite. Limited. Living in the natural world, I can only see and understand what occurs within my field of view. And the more fear is involved, the narrower that field of view becomes. Like a police officer or a soldier in a gunfight, the greater the fear, the more restricted the vision. Our bodily fight-or-flight response naturally causes us to focus more on the perceived threat, and tunnel vision occurs. We lose the ability to see what else is going on around us and in us. The greater the perceived threat, the narrower our vision becomes.

Whether we acknowledge it or not, we live in two very active worlds at the same time: the natural and the spiritual.

> *"... reality is far more extensive than our habitual perception of it."*
> – Eugene Peterson, *Run with the Horses*

All of us readily acknowledge the natural world. It's the world in which we breathe, rain falls, and we feel pain. It is what most people call "real." But as Christians, if we are to fully step into tov and the abundant life Jesus offers, we must acknowledge and engage the spiritual world as well, often both at the same time.

The spiritual world is the world in which angels and demons collide. The world where the Spirit of God moves with everything from physical healing to a tweak of the heart in the middle of the night that changes the course of your life. The crossover of the two is where we hear God speak. Feel God move. Experience the *"peace that transcends all understanding."*[61]

Jesus, knowing how conflicted we are as people living primarily in the post-Eden natural world, spoke boldly about fear and, thankfully, its antidote.

> *"Don't let your hearts be troubled. Trust in God, and trust also in me."* – John 14:1 NLT

> *"I have told you these things, so that in me you may have peace. In this world you will have trouble. But take heart! I have overcome the world."* – John 16:33

Jesus himself is the antidote to fear, accessed through trust. We may not see a solution or a way out. But Jesus tells us to trust in him all the same. No matter what. To trust in him without understanding.

As I said earlier, Paul learned that lesson and shared it with the Philippians when he said, *"For I can do everything through Christ, who gives me strength."*[62] Paul learned that in his natural experience of the world around him, there were things he could not see that limited his vision and threatened to create fear and anxiety. His antidote was to tap into the spiritual world for clarity. To lean into Jesus—without being able to understand rationally what was going on in his circumstances—for strength, courage, and rescue.

Regardless of the circumstances in your life, no matter what is going on in and around you in this natural world, I encourage you to lean into the mystery of your life and trust Jesus no matter what.

"Don't be afraid, for I am with you.
 Don't be discouraged, for I am your God.
 I will strengthen you and help you.
 I will hold you up with my righteous right hand."
– Isaiah 41:10

How you respond is your choice. You must choose to allow the mystery of God's unlimited ability to act on your behalf whether you understand how it works or not.

PART THREE

DISCOVERING GOD'S TOV HEART

CHAPTER 6
GOD THE GARDENER

"... I will make rivers flow on barren heights, and springs within the valleys. I will turn the desert into pools of water, and the parched ground into springs. I will put in the desert the cedar and the acacia, the myrtle and the olive. I will set junipers in the wasteland, the fir and the cypress together, so that people may see and know, may consider and understand, that the hand of the Lord has done this, that the Holy One of Israel has created it."

ISAIAH 41:18-20

THE MOST IMPORTANT THING

"The most important thing in your life is not what you do. It is who you become." – Dallas Willard

TOV MARKER

Change is inevitable. And yet there is one fixed point in the universe that never changes. God's love. As we struggle to keep our eyes fixed upon God's love, there are three words of rescue that will always lead you home – Eyes on Jesus. As you step out of the boat[63] and into the world around you, Eyes on Jesus. As you search for the tov heart and abundant life, the most important thing is to keep your eyes on Jesus.

We live today in a culture of change. And, not only change, but rapid change. The apps on our phone change. Our feelings change. The world around us changes, as do the people. Even the things that we believe to be firm and secure are sometimes not. Coastlines, mountains, forests, glaciers. Friends, pastors, teachers, parents. Everything we know in this world, at some point, changes. Sometimes slow, sometimes fast, but things are always in transition. Maybe that is why "someday" is such a dangerous word. Someday requires change, and we are already overwhelmed by change. We have way too much change in our lives, and we just don't like it.

Change is unsettling. Disturbing. And, at some level in

our soul, painful.

But we do have one fixed point of reference. A True North. A never-changing anchor upon which we can secure our hearts. God's love.

Give thanks to the Lord, for he is good.
His love endures forever.
Give thanks to the God of gods.
His love endures forever.
Give thanks to the Lord of lords:
His love endures forever.
– Psalm 136:1-3

In early November 2019, I was facilitating a church small group in our home. One day as I was praying about the group, Jesus said to me, *Eyes on me. Tell your group.* These three simple words became one of the biggest rescues of my life. *Eyes on me.*

Three months later, COVID and the resulting global tsunami of chaos hit with all the fear, fury, and animosity the world and the Evil One could muster.

But Jesus had provided a rescue, and over the course of the next two years, those three lifesaving words prevented catastrophe in my life and the lives of many around me.

Eyes on me.

These three words are now the cornerstone of my life. No matter what is going on in or around me. No matter my circumstances. Eyes on Jesus.

Peter was faced with the same choice when he stepped out of the boat:

Shortly before dawn Jesus went out to them, walking on the lake. When the disciples saw him walking on the lake, they were terrified. "It's a ghost," they said, and cried out in fear.

But Jesus immediately said to them: "Take courage! It is I. Don't be afraid."

"Lord, if it's you," Peter replied, "tell me to come to you on the water."

"Come," he said.

Then Peter got down out of the boat, walked on the water and came toward Jesus. But when he saw the wind, he was afraid and, beginning to sink, cried out, "Lord, save me!"

Immediately Jesus reached out his hand and caught him. "You of little faith," he said, "why did you doubt?"

And when they climbed into the boat, the wind died down. Then those who were in the boat worshiped him, saying, "Truly you are the Son of God."

– Matthew 14:25-33

When Peter kept his eyes on Jesus, even during a raging storm, he could do amazing things. When he didn't, well, we know how that story goes. Sinking fast and three denials before the cock crowed.

I know, not just in my head but deep in every corner of my heart, that God loves me and has me...no matter what.

God's love. If I keep my eyes on him.

God's love. If I choose it above all my other comforters.

God's love. Even when I can't see or don't understand.

The eternal, immovable presence of God's love is at the very heart of my walk with him. It is the most important thing that has moved from my head to my heart. It is the cornerstone of tov and abundant life. Eyes on Jesus in the context of God's love.

Paul understood this and staked his life on it. Not only that, but as we've already seen in another context, he gave it away as a prayer to his dear friends in Ephesus.

> *I pray that from his glorious, unlimited resources he will empower you with inner strength through his Spirit. Then Christ will make his home in your hearts as you trust in him. Your roots will grow down into God's love and keep you strong. And may you have the power to understand, as all God's people should, how wide, how long, how high, and how deep his love is. May you experience the love of Christ, though it is too great to understand fully. Then you will be made complete with all the fullness of life and power that comes from God.* - Ephesians 3:16-19 NLT

Another way to say, "*Eyes on Jesus*" is "*Trust Jesus..*"

On this journey, if you get to a ledge and you're afraid to take another step—trust Jesus. If you get to a sheer rock face that looks impossible to climb—trust Jesus. If you come to a raging river that appears too turbulent to cross—trust Jesus.

In joy or sorrow. In exultation or trauma. In current thought or memory. In dreams or nightmares. Trust Jesus. That trust crosses all barriers including time and space. And this trust is the only thing that can securely hold your heart no matter what. Trust Jesus...no matter what.

Remember my earlier scallop shell story? Those are the simple, beautiful events in your life that help the love of God move from your head to your heart. From intellectual assent to unshakable truth.

Also, remember that the events and stories of your life are different than mine. They are unique. Fearful and wonderful in their living. Don't compare my experience to yours. Jesus will meet you where you are, in who he created you to be. Look for them in your day-to-day.[64]

And don't forget to ask questions. I wouldn't have found the depth of God's love for me if I hadn't been inquisitive enough to asked Jesus the simple question, "*Is there a reason you're giving me scallop shells?*" Jesus wants to heal and renew your heart, but he rarely answers questions he's not asked. He likes to be asked.

In the C.S. Lewis book "*The Magician's Nephew,*"[65] the following conversation between Polly and the horse Sledge about Aslan, the Jesus character, is instructive.

Polly: "*Wouldn't he know without being asked?*"
The Horse: "*I've no doubt he would, but I've a sort of an idea he likes to be asked.*"

Jesus likes to be asked.

For the journey ahead, remember that your search for tov, the restoration of your heart, and Jesus' offer of abundant life are not metaphors or "*pie in the sky*" but a true way of life. A true way for you to live. Abundant life grounded in the flourishing creativity of the ever-flowing abundance and love of God. Tov. Your ability to fulfill both your design and purpose in the world. To create environments where life can flourish, for you and for others.

Buckle up, brother. Here we go!

THERE IS A WAY

There once was a man standing in a magnificent garden. A place full of life. A place where life flourished. But the man's story is about to go sideways. And so are the stories of his wife and children down through innumerable generations.

TOV MARKER
The Parable of the Sower provides a powerful framework for seeing our walk in the world, the affect and effect of the choices we make, and the work of God in and through our lives.

In chapter 13 of his Gospel, Matthew recounts one of Jesus' most famous parables, the Parable of the Sower. In it, Jesus describes four environments where seed can be planted both in our lives and the lives of others. Along the path, in rocky places, in thorny ground, and, lastly, in good soil. In this parable, the environment is your heart, and the seed is God's Word. Our experience of him in all its forms—Wisdom and Revelation. It is both his Word to us and that Word alive in us, working daily to restore tov in our hearts and lead us to abundant life.

This agricultural paradigm provides a good framework as we step into what it means to receive and recreate tov in our lives through the restoration of our heart. Not all environments are created equal. If you are to find abundant life, you must recognize these environments, how they express themselves in your life. How tov expresses itself in and through the Word of God as its foundation. And the renewal of your heart as you experience the love and mystery that is the work of God within you.

Leading to a harvest thirty, sixty, or one hundred times what was sown.

THE CASUAL ENVIRONMENT

"As he was scattering the seed, some fell along the path, and the birds came and ate it up." – Matthew 13:4

TOV MARKER

In the Casual Environment there is not an accidental or unintentional lack of understanding. It is contemptuous. A deliberate and purposeful refusal to understand and consider.

The first environment Jesus describes is what I will call the Casual Environment. I say "casual" because the seed of the Word and experience of God is placed in an environment that is quite casual. Think of casual like of when you tell someone something important, and they respond with "Whatever."

The unwillingness to understand or even consider your words demonstrates active contempt.

In verses 14 and 15 of Matthew 13, Jesus quotes the prophet Isaiah, saying,

"You will indeed hear but never understand, and you will indeed see but never perceive. For this people's heart has grown dull, and with their ears they can barely hear, and their eyes they have closed,

lest they should see with their eyes and hear with their ears and understand with their heart and turn, and I would heal them."

The implication here is that this Casual Environment is purposefully "dull" or "hardened."

This is not an accidental or unintentional lack of understanding. It is a deliberate and purposeful refusal to understand and consider. This is an environment where what has been planted is immediately dismissed. And so, through arrogance and pride the Evil One comes and steals what God has intentionally planted.

"The thief comes only to steal..." – John 10:10

THE HEAD ENVIRONMENT

"Some fell on rocky places, where it did not have much soil. It sprang up quickly, because the soil was shallow. But when the sun came up, the plants were scorched, and they withered because they had no root."
– Matthew 13:5-6

TOV MARKER
The Head Environment is a dry and desolate place. Wholly resistant to and incapable of receiving both the strength and nourishment of God's love.

Next is the Head Environment. This was my experience of Christianity for most of my life in the Church. A man steeped in twentieth-century intellectualism.

This is the environment where the Word and experience of God receives only intellectual assent. Where we say to ourselves, "*That's seems reasonable,*" or "*Yes, I agree with that,*" but we never allow the Word of God to become intimate, personal experience. The seed is never allowed to germinate and grow. Its roots fail to grow deep into God's love and move from our heads to our hearts because, as Jesus says, they "*have no root.*"

A plant is dead without its roots. The deeper a plant's roots grow, the more it can withstand the tossing, turning, and disruption of wind and storm. The better it is able to find nourishment and stand strong in times of drought.

In the same way, when our life with God has no root, we are easily taken out. But when our life with God is founded on his Word and grounded in his love in our hearts, our roots grow down deep into the nourishing assurance of his love. This is the place with him where we are able to withstand the storms of life when they come.

Jesus assumed there would be trials, what he termed "*tribulation or persecution.*" The wind and storms of life that work to unsettle us, distract us, and disrupt our comfort.

The Head Environment is a dry and desolate place, where we are incapable of receiving both the strength and nourishment of God's love.

In the Head Environment, there is no experience of God in the heart to back up the knowledge in our minds. So, when the inevitable problems of life come. Pain, opposition, anger, hatred, trauma, and oppression. What we "know" is easily cast aside for what we think is a simpler, less painful path. A path that seems to be easier for a time but ultimately bears no fruit, provides no comfort, and leaves us lost and alone. It is a place bereft of peace, hope, and, most importantly, love.

Years of frustration, searching for love
Striving so hard I could not see
All of the while you're right there beside me
Calling me to all I could be

Buried in the pages of all the right books
Wanting a you that I can see
Praying to the gods of intellect and wisdom
But it's not in my mind that I'm set free

Because it's not in my mind at all
But in my heart is where I fall
Not in my mind but in my heart
Is where I fall in love with you[66]

But I want to be absolutely clear here. Deep relationship with God is not either/or. Head or heart. But, often the gateway to our heart and the deep assurance of God is through our mind. Which is why the Apostle Paul tells us in Romans:

"Do not conform to the pattern of this world, but be transformed by the renewing of your mind. Then you will be able to test and approve what God's will is—his good, pleasing and perfect will." – Romans 12:2

It is the "patterns of our world" that confound us today and separate us from our heart. We are told that science is the only arbiter of truth; when in reality, scientific "truth" changes almost daily. Just wait a bit. The next study, survey, or experiment will disprove what was previously held as being true.

The mind and the heart must work together to experience the fullness of our relationship with each member of the trinity. It is when we leave the heart to graze in the pasture of our life, disconnected from what we know to be true, that we stumble around lost in the Head Environment.

THE THORNY ENVIRONMENT

"Other seed fell among thorns, which grew up and choked the plants."
– Matthew 13:7

TOV MARKER

In a Thorny Environment we become distracted by the worries and cares of life. Or get so comfortable with wealth that we step away from our reliance and dependence on God. And, like Peter, begin to sink. Drowning in the sea of the world's anxiety, fear, and anger. Or, its frustration, pride, arrogance, and complacency.

The third environment Jesus addresses is the Thorny Environment. The Word and experience of God dropped into this environment takes root and grows quickly. We receive it with joy, even wonder.

However, because there are *"thorns"* also planted here, life is suppressed and stifled by the world.

The world is the culture we live in. It is anything that entices you to put your hope in or reliance on anything other than God. So, when we take our eyes off Jesus, we are easily distracted and confused.

Think of Peter in Matthew 14, as we talked about earlier. Jesus comes to the disciples walking on the water and tells them not to be afraid.

Peter wants confirmation that it is truly Jesus, and Jesus says, "*Come*." Peter steps out of the boat and walks on the water toward Jesus. But quickly he sees the "*thorns*." He is distracted by the wind, by the circumstances of his life, and his gaze shifts. He takes his eyes off Jesus. The result of that shift? He begins to sink.

Peter is not a "*bad*" man. He is a man who has grown up in the world of the practical. A man who is now learning to deal with the God of the universe who told him simply to "*come*."

In the same way, when we become distracted by the worries and cares of life or get so comfortable with wealth that we step away from our reliance and dependence on God, we, like Peter, begin to sink and drown in the sea of the world's anxiety, fear, anger, and frustration or its pride, arrogance, and complacency. We are choked off from the source of life, and we become unfruitful.

I experienced this environment firsthand when I let the abundance and provision of God go to my head. He had provided me with a job that paid me well into the six figures. Like Peter, I wasn't a "*bad*" man. But I took the provision for granted and wasted it. Like the prodigal son, I squandered it. Not on sex, drugs, and rock and roll, but in complacency and arrogance. As a result, I nearly lost everything I held dear. All because I took my eyes off Jesus and let the worries and cares of life mute and limit my experience of God.

THE TOV ENVIRONMENT

"Still other seed fell on good soil, where it produced a crop—a hundred, sixty or thirty times what was sown." – Matthew 13:8

TOV MARKER

The Tov Environment is the place where God's Word and our experience of him are planted together in the good soil of God's steadfast love. There we bear fruit that yields a crop thirty, sixty, or a hundred times what was sown.

Last environment Jesus addresses is the Tov Environment. This is the environment that Jesus calls "good soil." The antithesis of the previous three environments.

A place where we look for more of God. Where we experience, not just know, God's love. And, where the worries and cares of life pale in comparison to the abundance and provision he gives every day.

Where in the Casual Environment there is not only no understanding but no desire to understand, active contempt. Here, we *"seek first the kingdom of God and his righteousness."*[67]

Where in the Head Environment there is only intellectual assent. Here we are intellectually transformed by the renewing of our minds.[68] And, go even further to experience the fullness of God's love that surpasses knowledge.[69]

Where in the Thorny Environment we become easily distracted by the worries and cares the world throws at us or the blessings God bestows. Here we keep our eyes fixed on Jesus, *"the author and perfecter of our faith,"*[70] *"so that we may be one with him as he is one with the Father."*[71] *"A firm and secure anchor for our souls."*[72]

Eyes on Jesus.

The Tov Environment is the place where God's Word and our experience of him are planted together in the good soil of God's steadfast love. Bearing fruit that yields a crop thirty, sixty, or a hundred times what was originally sown. Abundant life. This, my friends, is the environment where life can flourish. This is the Tov Environment. This is the only place where we and those around us have the opportunity to be all God created us to be.

But there are obstacles to the creation of this environment.[73] There are choices we must make and work we must do for God to transform our hearts into *"good soil."*

The Tov Environment is God's recreation of Eden within us, in our hearts.

It is his desire for each of us.

But you must be willing and determined like Jesus.[74] Setting yourself as resolutely toward him as Jesus did toward Jerusalem and the cross.

You can be all God created you to be and create environments in and around you where life can flourish.

But first you must do some farming. And to farm, you must accept and engage the process.

CHAPTER 7
SOWING TOV

"Do not be deceived: God cannot be mocked. A man reaps what he sows. Whoever sows to please their flesh, from the flesh will reap destruction; whoever sows to please the Spirit, from the Spirit will reap eternal life."

GALATIANS 6:7-8

THE TOV PROCESS

"It is for freedom that Christ has set us free." – Galatians 5:1

TOV MARKER

The tov process is written into the fabric of this world by God himself. It is one of the strongest reasons for hope in the world. It is also not on a "one size fits all" timeline. God knows what needs accomplishing to make your heart fertile and that often takes time. He wants to do this work with you. He must do it with you. He will not do it against your will. You cannot compromise the process.

In the Parable of the Sower, Jesus presents us with not only the parable itself but also the interpretation and application. It is the application of this parable that is crucial to understanding how God works within you, with you, and through you to create the Tov Environment in your heart.

The picture here is a simple one that Jesus' listeners would have easily grasped. It is also a framework easily understood by any farmer. Unfortunately, the meaning of this imagery is lost to most people in today's Western industrial-technical world.

Seeds hold the stuff of life, the essence and the being of life. They are the everyday expression of tov in the world, created that way by the hand of God. However, for that "stuff" to be released and life to flourish, a process must take place.

Germination. The process of germination is an accurate mirror of the tov process of our heart.

It is only in and through the process of germination of the seed that the plant flourishes, bears fruit and creates more plants. This is the tov process in nature.

For a seed to become a plant and flourish, bearing more seeds and creating more life, the right events must occur, in the right order. It is a simple process[75] consisting of:

- *Water*
- *Time*
- *Chilling*
- *Warming*
- *Oxygen*
- *Light*

We see this demonstrated abundantly in nature. What happens when an area of ground is left alone? Plants grow. Life is the basic tenet of the world as created by God. It is built into the world and cannot be permanently stopped.

The process can be hindered and opposed. A field can be sprayed with Roundup, killing everything in it. But given time, the plants will return and overtake the field.

The same is true of forest fires. Everything, from trees to grass, can burn to basic carbon across vast stretches of land, but it won't be too long before life returns.

The tov process is written into the fabric of this world by God himself. It is one of the strongest reasons for hope in the world. Everything in this world ultimately can and will grow. And, if properly tended, flourish.

But we live outside Eden in a land parched and dry. Weeds and thorns also grow. Often it seems, better and faster than fruit and flowers, vegetables and trees. Without the right environment and care, germination cannot take place. The seed rots and dies, bearing no fruit.

Because of *The Fall*, the earth often requires human assistance to flourish, bear fruit, and multiply. This was God's call on man in the beginning,[76] what we call farming.

That is why gardens must be tended and, the garden of your heart is no different.

The process of transforming your heart into a fertile tov environment where life can flourish is also simple. Requiring events to occur in the right order.

- *Love, support, and encouragement*
- *Consistency*
- *Space for growth*
- *The reassurance of love, support, and encouragement*
- *Hope*
- *The presence of God*

But while the tov process in and of itself is simple, it too requires assistance to flourish, bear fruit, and multiply. This assistance comes primarily through the actions of others, our own actions, and the work of God through the Holy Spirit.

Through the actions of others, we are introduced to God and his work. We are also supported and encouraged in his work.

Through our own actions, we submit to the IF in God's Word, obey, and live out of the resulting abundance. We also take fierce mastery over our will. Transforming the unintentional, coasting way of life into one of strength and intention.

Through the work of God in us, we become open to the mysterious, holy, redemptive power of the Holy Spirit to transform arid ground into fertile soil for planting.

This process may be rapid, or it may take time. It's often a combination of both. There are times in our lives when we grow and flourish with amazing speed. There are also times when growth seems to take "forever."

If it takes time, you are not "blowing it." All it means is that it takes time. God's work in our lives is his own, and he sees and knows us better than we know ourselves. Much better.

The tov process is not on a "one size fits all" timeline. He knows what needs to be done to make your heart fertile. He knows the dry, hardened places in your heart caused by your wounds, your brokenness, your pain, and your sin. He knows what your head has buried. The things you have experienced that you don't remember because you don't want to. The things you can't remember because they would be too painful to bear. He knows the things you have done or not done that require forgiveness, both his and yours. Yes, Jesus knows, and he wants to set you free!

He doesn't want to just give you a Band-Aid. Sometimes tending these places in your heart will take minor nursing. Sometimes they will require major surgery. But he wants you truly healed, renewed, and redeemed.

> *"The Spirit of the Lord is on me, because...he has sent me to proclaim freedom for the prisoners and recovery of sight for the blind, to set the oppressed free..."* – Luke 4:18

And he wants to do this work *with* you. He must do it with you. He will not do it against your will. There is no "magic bullet" or formula. Everyone's path is unique and singular. There is no other way.

But the process is the same and you must be an active participant. It is the tov process of your redemption, healing, and renewal. And Jesus will not compromise the process.

Remember Yvon Chouinard's words, "...*if you compromise the process, you're an asshole when you start out and an asshole when you get back.*"

LOVE, SUPPORT, AND ENCOURAGEMENT

"*And now these three remain: faith, hope and love. But the greatest of these is love.*" – 1 Corinthians 13:13

"*Encouragement is like water to the soul; it makes everything grow.*"
– Chris Burkmenn

TOV MARKER

In germination it is water that is the necessary catalyst to allow a seed to rehydrate, become permeable, and begin to grow. The same is true of our lives. It is our experience of the love, support, and encouragement of God and others that opens our hearts to the movement of God toward tov.

For a seed to begin to germinate, it must absorb water. Water, being the source of life, must permeate the seed to rehydrate the seed's cells.

Note that the seed's cells are not dead. They are simply dormant. The same is true of your heart. It may feel deadlocked away, buried, shut down—but it's not. God wants to awaken it. He wants to bring tov to your heart!

For you to begin to become who God created you to be, you must be saturated with love, support, and encouragement. Life just doesn't happen or magically appear. This saturation must take place so that your heart can be open to the possibility of life. Nourishing your inner places of dryness. Places locked away and protected from the pain and trauma of the world and the devastating effect of sin—both yours and others—must first be watered. Your heart must experience love, support, and encouragement. The writer of Hebrews understood how important this is:

> "But encourage one another daily, as long as it is called 'Today,' so that none of you may be hardened by sin's deceitfulness."
> – Hebrews 3:13

> "And let us consider how we may spur one another on toward love and good deeds." – Hebrews 10:24

The initial impact of love, support, and encouragement begins the process that softens and opens your heart up to God and to others.

This is why isolation is so deadly and why it is one of the Evil One's most powerful tools. Our isolation is not just physical. Often, we appear physically present and yet our hearts are locked way. Emotional isolation is just as deadly, maybe more so. Whenever we shut ourselves off from others it is a recipe for disaster.

You can only experience love, support, and encouragement in the context of others. Ideally, in the context of Christian community.

We'll discuss Christian community in more depth later. But for now, simply recognize the way God works in and through those who deeply love him and seek to be in close, committed union with him.[77] Your heart being nourished and renewed through the living water of Jesus flowing through them into the world.[78]

To be clear, Christian community is not only found in a church you attend. My Christian community is wide and varied. Some of my deepest, most encouraging and supportive relationships are outside the church I attend. They are my allies nonetheless, they have my back, and I have theirs. There is one beautiful, powerful thing they have in common—a passion for Jesus and union with him. If you're not there yet, take heart! If you really want it, you will find it and, one day, that will be you. Your life overflowing into the lives of others.

CONSISTENCY OVER TIME

"Live in the day, measure in the decade."[79] – Morgan Snyder

TOV MARKER

It takes time for a seed to absorb water. To become hydrated and ready to grow. Our hearts are the same. The worries and cares of life, along with sin, and the attack of the Evil One, harden our hearts. Time is needed for the love, support, and encouragement of God and others to soften your heart. To prepare it for tov.

Time must be allowed for a seed to absorb water. It takes time for things that are hard and dry, including seeds and hearts, to become moist and pliable. Open to life.

It is love, support, and encouragement that soften the heart. Nurturing our hearts and providing the conditions where your heart can become open to freedom and life. But it takes time.

This is as true of your heart as it is of seeds planted in a garden. Real freedom rarely takes place in an instant. Sometimes it does but most often it takes weeks, months, and sometimes years.

Becoming receptive to the work of God in our lives takes time. And most importantly, the constancy of love, support, and encouragement. That is why we as God's children are called to love others. And not just once, but over and over and over.

> *"Then Peter came to Jesus and asked, 'Lord, how many times shall I forgive my brother or sister who sins against me? Up to seven times?'*
>
> *Jesus answered, 'I tell you, not seven times, but seventy-seven times.'"* – Matthew 18:21-22

Unfortunately, most of us are impatient. We live in an internet-fueled, streaming, fast-food culture. We do everything on the go and, if we are honest, we waste our most precious resource: time. There is an old saying that went, "Good things come to those who wait." The Bible itself speaks volumes about waiting on God.

> *"Wait for the Lord; be strong, and let your heart take courage; wait for the Lord!"* – Psalm 27:14

THE TOV HEART

"But they who wait for the Lord shall renew their strength; they shall mount up with wings like eagles; they shall run and not be weary; they shall walk and not faint." – Isaiah 40:31

"The Lord is good to those who wait for him, to the soul who seeks him." – Lamentations 3:25

We must lean into the love, support, and encouragement God is providing over time. Letting it soften our hearts. Preparing us for the abundant life to come. Preparing us for tov.

ALLOWING SPACE FOR GROWTH

"To be or not to be, that is the question."
– William Shakespeare, *Hamlet*

TOV MARKER
Failing a period of chilling, a seed may fail to germinate and grow to its full potential. For us, our hearts need space. Space grounded not in the expectation of service but the expectancy of God's work in our lives. The space to discover and begin to become who he created to us be.

Many seeds will not germinate unless they experience a period of low temperature. Failing this "chilling," germination may fail or be significantly delayed.

In the same way, we must allow space for growth. Space that, while still existing in the presence of love, support, and encouragement, allows us to establish who we truly are in the context of that love and God's work in our lives. This is a space without pressure to be, act, or respond in a certain way. The space of stepping back slightly to allow ourselves to survey the trail ahead. Space where we lean not into expectation but expectancy.

Expectation is grounded in self—what is expected of you or what you expect of yourself. Expectancy is grounded in the unknown of what God is going to do within the context of his love.

This is NOT the person you want to be, or the person others say you should be. This is the person God, in the fullness of his love, uniquely created you to be.

Too often in the church, we are told to be who the church wants or needs us to be before we have discovered God's intent for us.

In 2017, after many decades of being useful in the church serving and leading groups, I was burned out. Then, in a beautiful rescue, God gave me permission to step back and experience him for a season. Discovering where he wanted to use me.

I still went to church, engaged in my small group, and cared for others. But I had no visible "status" under the church banner of ministry. It was there, in this season of being "invisible", that I rested. It was here that he showed me to the place of true service he wanted for me in the church. This beautiful season of rest lasted for about two years. I don't know if that was long or short, but it was what I needed, and it is what the church needed too.

When I stepped back into official, "visible" ministry, it was into fostering prayer within the church. Was it powerful and anointed? Not in a worldly sense. But I planted and watered a seed, a seed that continues to grow and flourish.

We must all take time to be. There is much organizational need in the Western church today. Too often we are thrown or coerced into "ministry" simply because there is a need. We are there and can do a job. An organizational job that becomes what many call ministry.

It is here where, too often, we miss our true calling. The place where God desires to impact the world through us, because we get busy. Busy with life, busy with church, busy with "stuff."

Don't get me wrong. "Stuff" can be good, and there is a lot of good "stuff" we can do, especially in the church. But not all good stuff is God stuff. And as we are seeking tov, the best stuff is God stuff. The stuff that brings life, freedom, and growth.

Maybe that's what Shakespeare was thinking when he wrote: *"To be or not to be, that is the question."*

REASSURANCE

"Our highest assurance of the goodness of Providence seems to me to rest in the flowers. It is only goodness which gives extras, and so I say again we have much to hope for from the flowers."
– Sherlock Holmes, *The Naval Treaty*[80]

TOV MARKER
Following the time of chilling is a time of warming in which the plant itself emerges and begins to grow. The same is true for our hearts and lives as we step lightly into tov and the seedlings of abundant life. But, like young emerging plants, we are tender and vulnerable. Those who knew us previously will continue to try to define us by who we were. We ourselves, in shame and guilt, will be tempted by the Evil One to do the same. It is during this season that we must especially guard our hearts and remember to keep our Eyes on Jesus.

The next step in germination is a period of warming. Spurring growth and facilitating the emergence of the plant itself.

It is reassurance that facilitates the emergence of our initial steps toward life and renewal of our tov hearts.

During this time, our hearts, like plants, are tender, delicate, and susceptible to damage. We must be careful with our interpretation and guard against misunderstanding. During this time, we are our most vulnerable. Vulnerable to hurt, disappointment, diminishment, and a return to isolation.

It is often here in your walk with God that "the church" willfully or accidentally wounds your heart. It is here that you must remember that you are a follower of Christ, not of any Christian. It is here that you must remember that Christians are still recovering fallen beings. Those around you in the church can and will make mistakes. They are human and so, like you, they will sin. But it is the grace God showed you on the cross that provides the context and strength for the grace you can bestow both on others and yourself.

Jesus spoke often about forgiveness. It is here during this time of reassurance that you may truly learn what it means to forgive.

During this time of reassurance, you will also begin to learn balance and what it means to truly love. Chuck Swindoll once said, *"Love is a great river bounded by discernment and truth."*

In the balance between truth and discernment, life and death, forgiveness and anger, you learn to love both God and others. Jesus was the most balanced man who has ever lived. He showed you what is possible, and how you are to live with others.

Jesus showed you that you can be angry and not vengeful. That you can love with strength and true compassion without appeasement. That you can care deeply and passionately without additional burden.

It is reassurance, the continuance of love, support, and encouragement, both from God and others, that provides the covering and protection required when the realities of living in a broken world come crashing in. Through sin and the attempts of the Evil One to "steal, kill, and destroy."

Every movement toward God will be opposed. And depending on your story—your brokenness and wounds, your sin and the sin of others—the work of God toward the recovery of the tov heart and abundant life will be challenged.

This is the primary reason King Solomon gave this counsel,

> "*Above all else, guard your heart, for it is the wellspring of life.*"
> - Proverbs 4:23 NIV 1984

You must guard your heart. If you want tov and the abundant life, you must protect your heart. Not in the sense of locking it up and shutting it down but guarding it and leaning into what is true. That you are seen, known, and deeply and passionately loved.

And you must resist and renounce the lies of the Evil One through shame and guilt. Lies that you are not worthy, too broken, or unlovable.

Remember, you now find your life, purpose, and strength not in people or things but in God—Father, Jesus, Holy Spirit. You are not who you were.

> "*Therefore, if anyone is in Christ, he is a new creation.*
> *The old has passed away; behold, the new has come*"
> - 2 Corinthians 5:17 NIV 1984

This is one of the hardest truths in Scripture, but you absolutely must hold on to it. Your past informs your story, but it is not the end of it. Your past is who you were, not who you are. Your past is not to be locked away, never to be seen again.

It is through your past that God intends to impact the world.

In the series *The Chosen*, there is a beautiful conversation between Phillip and Matthew that illustrates this truth.[81]

> **Phillip:** "*I was something else once, too. Once you've met the Messiah, 'am' is all that matters. Next time he rides you, remind him that the people out there want to define us by our past. Our sins.*"
> **Matthew:** "*Out there, where?*"
> **Phillip:** "*With the sleepers. But we're different, we're awake. Everybody in your old life is playing a different game than you. Do you get it?*"

Do you get it? You are NOT who you were. You are who you are. You are seen, you are known, and you are deeply and passionately loved by the creator of the universe! Always have been. Always will be. And your deepest, fullest reassurance of this is found when you keep your *Eyes on Jesus*.

No matter what!

HOPE & FAITH

"May the God of hope fill you with all joy and peace as you trust in him, so that you may overflow with hope by the power of the Holy Spirit."
– Romans 15:13

TOV MARKER

For a seed, it is oxygen that provides the fuel to spur growth. For us, that fuel is hope and faith. The nourishment of the tov heart and abundant life in plenty and in need. No matter what.

Oxygen is the fuel that spurs a seed's growth. With continued water, time, and warming, the presence of oxygen ensures that the seed will continue to germinate and flourish.

As people created in the image of God, hope and its close cousin faith is our fuel. Hope and faith are the oxygen of our lives that accelerates our growth as we begin to put down roots into the fertile soil of God's love.

"'For I know the plans I have for you,' declares the Lord, 'plans to prosper you and not to harm you, plans to give you hope and a future.'" – Jeremiah 29:11

"Blessed be the God and Father of our Lord Jesus Christ! According to his great mercy, he has caused us to be born again to a living hope through the resurrection of Jesus Christ from the dead."
– 1 Peter 1:3

> "*God did this so that, by two unchangeable things in which it is impossible for God to lie, we who have fled to take hold of the hope set before us may be greatly encouraged. We have this hope as an anchor for the soul, firm and secure.*" – Hebrews 6:18-19a

Hope is the foundation of faith. And it is faith that fuels God's work in us, no matter our circumstances. The continuation of life in the face of death. The continuation of life in the face of the false gods of pleasure, wealth, and power.

Too often our hope and faith are small and weak because they have become grounded in ourselves. What we can make happen, what we can see becoming reality.

If your hope and faith are grounded in what you are capable of, you will fail to bear fruit. Tov snuffed out like the extinguishing of a fire by oxygen deprivation.

But the writer of Hebrews shows us a different way. A way that fans into flame the spark of tov in our heart. And, where for us they are simply hopes and dreams, for God they are creation and intention.

> "*Now faith is being sure of what we hope for and certain of what we do not see.*" – Hebrews 11:1

He defines true faith, tov faith, as faith grounded in the hope of what God is capable of. Hope that is limitless, powerful, and yes, dangerous.

> "*Hope: It is the only thing stronger than fear. A little hope is effective; a lot of hope is dangerous.*"
> – President Snow, *The Hunger Games: Catching Fire*

It is the blossoming of hope and faith, sending their roots deep into the love of God, that forms the bedrock of the tov heart and abundant life within us. More than we can dream or imagine.[82]

THE PRESENCE OF GOD

"If I say, 'Surely the darkness shall cover me, and the light about me be night,' even the darkness is not dark to you; the night is bright as the day, for darkness is as light with you." – Psalm 139:11-12

TOV MARKER

Exposure to light is the final step in germination, sparking the plant's prolonged and sustained growth. For us, this is the presence of God. God with us and in us, working through us to restore the tov heart in us. Enabling us to live out the abundant life in the overflow of his generosity and love.

The final step in the germination process is exposure to light. Light provides the bursting forth of leaves, buds, blossoms, flowers, fruit, and, ultimately, seeds. The creation of more life. Tov.

As people created in the image of God, we become all that God called us to be when we step into his presence. Relying completely on him, seeking him above all else, and finding our rest and restoration in him. It is his presence in our lives that provides the light we need to be tov. To flourish and to bear much fruit. To live out of who he created us to be.

So, what does it mean to experience the presence of God? To be in the presence of God is to be where he is.

The presence of God was first over the face of the deep. Then in the Garden of Eden, walking with Adam and later, Eve. It went before Moses into the Red Sea. It was where Moses went to receive the Ten Commandments. Angels stand in God's presence.[83] It is where ultimate judgment occurs.[84] And, it is a place of blessing.[85]

The presence of God brings strength and courage[86] and is something we cannot escape.[87] It is also the presence of God that provides rest, guidance, peace, and comfort. The presence of God is also manifest, made real to us, in the Trinitarian person of Holy Spirit.[88] Jesus himself tells Phillip that when we experience him, Jesus, we are also in the presence of the Father.[89] And he says that he himself will also be with us.[90]

It is in and through the glorious mystery that is the Trinity, that we are always and forever in the presence of God. Father, Jesus, Holy Spirit. In the presence of God, we are judged and receive grace. In the presence of God, we receive comfort, peace, and strength. In the presence of God, we receive protection, mercy, and love. And in the presence of God, we live out of his abundance. The overflowing generosity that creates within us the tov heart. Enabling us to live abundantly. For in God, there is no darkness, only light!

> "*This is the message we have heard from him and declare to you: God is light; in him there is no darkness at all.*" – 1 John 1:5

The light of God's presence enables you to be who he intended when he created you. It gives you the ability, if you choose it, to burst forth with life, love, and glory. This is the glory he intended to impact the world with when he created you. The overflowing of his presence within you. From the reservoir of his presence in your life, it brings forth more life, yielding a harvest thirty, sixty, one hundred times what was sown. And so, we pray:

> *Create in me a tov heart, O God. Father me in and through the generosity[91] that flows out of your abundance. Lord Jesus, teach me to care for myself and others in and through the love[92] that flows out of your abundance. Holy Spirit, fill me with the wisdom, discernment, comfort, strength, peace, and joy[93] that flow out of your abundance. Create in me a tov heart, O God, that I might live as you intended when you created me. Creating environments that flourish. Able to live the abundant life Jesus promised was available to me.[94] Amen!*

PART FOUR

AWAKENING THE TOV HEART

CHAPTER 8
GOD MATH

*Your redeemed story
plus your redeemed gifting,
in the context of God's love,
is the glory he wants to impact the world with.*

WAY OF THE KINGDOM

"For the Kingdom of God is not just a lot of talk; it is living by God's power." – 1 Corinthians 4:20 NLT

TOV MARKER

The way of the Kingdom of God, the way Jesus calls us to, is not the way of the world. The way of the world keeps us playing defense. Protecting what we have and who we think we should be. The way of the Kingdom of God is one where we live Alive, Full, and Free. Where your redeemed story plus your redeemed gifting, in the context of God's love, is the glory he uses to impact the world - God Math.

The way the Kingdom of God works has always been different from the way of this world.

The way of the world keeps us in protection mode, guarding what we have, the status quo. Our homes, our families, our work, our money, our health, our comfort, our...

Take a step back and answer the following question as honestly as you can:

What is it that you are protecting above everything else?

We are tenacious about it too and will stop at nothing to secure what we have acquired. That is the way of the world. To collect things, secure happiness, and then go on defense. Even in addiction, war, and the brutality of every form of abuse and trauma. We are always focused to a single end, our own happiness.

> *All men seek happiness. This is without exception. Whatever different means they employ, they all tend to this end. The cause of some going to war, and of others avoiding it, is the same desire in both, attended with different views. The will never takes the least step but to this object. This is the motive of every action of every man, even of those who hang themselves.*
> – Blaise Pascal, *Pensées*[95]

Normally we are blind to it, but when we seek our own happiness, we develop the heart posture of striving. Which, at its core is to live life apart from God. It is the posture that says, *"This is all up to me."* and *"I have to make it happen."*

By nature, to be on defense is to worry. As we strive, plan, and scheme to secure happiness, we worry about how we're going to make that happen. This is our human nature: fallen, weak, and self-absorbed.

Jesus makes it clear that the way of the Kingdom is different. He wants us to make a shift. To shift our gazes and our hearts from this world to the Kingdom of God.

> *"Therefore I tell you, do not worry about your life, what you will eat or drink; or about your body, what you will wear. Is not life more than food, and the body more than clothes? Look at the birds of the air; they do not sow or reap or store away in barns, and yet your heavenly Father feeds them. Are you not much more valuable than they?"* – Matthew 6:25-26

He also provided us with a stern warning about focusing on the things of the world. The things in and of the world upon which we have grounded our happiness and our hope.

> "*Remember Lot's wife! Whoever tries to keep their life will lose it, and whoever loses their life will preserve it.*" – Luke 17:32-33

You cannot find tov and the abundant life if you are on the defensive. If you worry and strive. It is impossible. You must learn to live differently. To live Alive! Full! Free!

- **Alive** – To live in anticipation. To engage life in the fullness of creation. To live in the expectancy of what is possible and the goodness to come regardless of current circumstances.

- **Full** – To embrace the glory God has created in you. The glory you were meant to impact the world with, and which has been assaulted. To allow everyone you encounter to feel the weight of your glory with integrity and truth.

- **Free** – To engage others squarely centered in both your glory and God's love, no matter how they may be opposed. To boldly answer God's question, "*Is your fear greater than my love?*" with a resounding "*NO!*"

The Apostle Paul put it this way:

> "*Do not conform to the pattern of this world, but be transformed by the renewing of your mind. Then you will be able to test and approve what God's will is—his good, pleasing and perfect will.*" – Romans 12:2

This doesn't mean we give up and move to complacency or ambivalence. We must still act, live, and move within the physical world we live in. The difference is in *how* we live. How we act, react, move, and, most importantly, who leads the charge.

In the movie *Kingdom of Heaven*,[96] as Balian's father is dying, he gives Balian an oath to live by. A new way of living beyond himself and in a story much larger than his own.

> "*Be without fear in the face of your enemies. Be brave and upright, that God may love thee. Speak the truth always, even if it leads to your death. Safeguard the helpless and do no wrong. That is your oath.*"

You are called to live open and free. Not protecting what you have but giving it all away, including the most important thing you own—yourself. Who you were, who you are, and who you are becoming.

It is in and through your story and gifting that you become the man God intended you to be. The man who is not ashamed or afraid of who he was. The man who knows and leans into his gifting for good. The man who has given up everything to keep his eyes on Jesus. The man who lives and loves in the context of God's love flowing out of the abundance of his union with God. A man, as Morgan Snyder puts it, *with nothing to hide, nothing to fear, and nothing to prove.*

This is God Math.

Your redeemed story plus your redeemed gifting, in the context of God's love, is the glory he wants to impact the world with.

The man living from his tov heart. Living the abundant life Jesus promised. This is the man who has learned to create environments for himself and others where life can flourish.

This is the way of the Kingdom.

YOUR LIFE IS STORY

"So take seriously the story that God has given you to live. It's time to read your own life, because your story is the one that could set us all ablaze." – Dan Allender, *To Be Told*[97]

TOV MARKER

Your life is a story. A narrative of your days on earth. It is also problematic because most of us don't really know our story and so are unable to share it with others. Also, we stuff much of it, the parts we don't like – hidden, tucked away, forgotten. But, to know your story and find redemption in and through it, you must go there with Jesus. The process can be painful, but it is in and through your story that your heart becomes tov.

Your life is not a set of random events taking place in time.

You live your life, in all its color, flavor, boredom, and boldness, as narrative, as a story. A narrative of your days on earth. Over time, the events of your life are woven together into a tapestry of shadow and light, sorrow and joy, disappointment and hope. Obviously, if you're reading this book, your story is not over. There is more to be written, more to be experienced, and more to be shared.

One of the two major problems we have as men is that, while we live in story, we are not comfortable with our story; either acknowledging or sharing it. As you are aware, women are much better at story than we are. Consider a trip to the grocery store for milk and bread.

> **Adam:** *"I went to the store and got milk and bread."*
> **Eve:** *"I got in my car and realized I didn't have my keys, so I had to go back in the house to get them. Oh, and by the way, the car was low on gas, so I stopped by the gas station on the way, and you'll never guess who I ran into ..."*

Exaggeration? Maybe a bit, but you get the picture. You live it. The problem here is that there really is more to be said in a man's story. Much more. We just don't acknowledge it. The result is that we have a hard time even knowing our own story, much less telling it to someone else.

The second major problem we have regarding story is that we take our cue from Adam and hide.

> *"But the Lord God called to the man, 'Where are you?' He answered, 'I heard you in the garden, and I was afraid because I was naked; so I hid.'"* – Genesis 3:9-10

THE TOV HEART

We have stuffed, ignored, hidden, and forgotten much of our story. But it is those things we have stuffed, ignored, hidden, and forgotten that return, seemingly out of nowhere, to disrupt our lives and the lives of those around us.

Like the surprise blowup at your wife or girlfriend, the kids, a neighbor, or a colleague. Afterward, we are confused and embarrassed, diminished and unsure. Most often, we just stuff, ignore, hide, or forget it...again. If we are smart, we ask ourselves, *"Where did that come from?"* If we are wise, we ask God, *"Where did that come from?"*

As the old saying goes, *"Nip it in the bud."* Meaning, address something while it's small before it becomes a larger issue. Your story needs to be *"fleshed out,"* made real, acknowledged, and redeemed. I will say more on redemption later, but for now, understand that there is more to your story than you have let yourself believe. It is more important than the world has let on. And it is more powerful than the Evil One wants you to know.

Your story also has characters. There are leading roles, and there are supporting characters.

In the movie *The Holiday*,[98] we glimpse the interwoven stories of five desperate people. One of the lead characters, Iris, is on holiday (vacation) from the UK to LA. She does a home swap with another lead character and ends up in a grand home in Beverly Hills. An old Hollywood screenwriter, Arthur Abbott, happens to live next door. When I say old, he was screenwriting in the Hollywood heyday of the 1940s and 1950s.

They become friends. And one night at dinner, Arthur, who has noticed some issues in Iris' life, calls her out, as good friends should.

Arthur: "*Iris, in the movies we have leading ladies, and we have the best friend. You, I can tell, are leading lady, but for some reason you're behaving like the best friend.*"

Iris: "*You're so right. You're supposed to be the leading lady of your own life, for God's sake. Arthur, I've been going to a therapist for three years and she's never explained anything to me that well. That was brilliant. Brutal but brilliant. Thank you.*"

Many of us are playing the wrong part in our stories, and our hearts have become casual, heady, or thorny. As a result, we fail to grow, flourish, and bear fruit. The good news is that you don't need to live that way. But if you are to bear fruit and live abundantly, you must learn to farm the soil of your heart. And that happens through your story.

This farming will take some hard work. As any farmer will tell you, farming is really hard work. But the farming of your heart occurs through the redemption of your story. It is hard work. Not in the sense that the work itself is innately hard but because it is often painful. And, because we don't like pain, we try to avoid it, push against it, make it hard.

But, if you go there with Jesus, his yoke is easy.[99] His work in and through you is some of the most rewarding and fulfilling work you will ever participate in. If you are willing to step into the work of knowing and healing your story with Jesus, the soil of your heart can become tov. Producing a crop, "a hundred, sixty or thirty times what was sown." It is in and through your story that your heart becomes tov.

ACCEPTING REDEMPTION

"Redemption involves deliverance from bondage based on the payment of a price by a redeemer." – Baker's Evangelical Dictionary[100]

TOV MARKER
The redemption provided by the Lord Jesus Christ on the cross is powerful and effective. However, for us to experience the fruit of that redemption, we must accept it. Even for those of us who have accepted the redemption of our sin, more is available.

Typical discussions of biblical redemption rightly focus on our redemption from sin (the bondage) by the work of the cross (the price paid) by Jesus of Nazareth (the redeemer). While this is a true and fundamental foundation for our walk with Christ, there is more. As we dive deeper into life with God in the context of tov, there is a further work of redemption in and through our stories—your story.

For most of us, even after our initial step into faith and the acknowledgment of the redemption of our sin, our stories remain in bondage.

I want to be very clear here. This bondage does not mean that the work of Jesus Christ is ineffective. On the contrary, the work of Christ to accomplish our redemption was fully effective on the cross when Jesus pronounced, *"It is finished."*[101]

However, while the work of Jesus on the cross was immediately and for all time effective, not everyone accepts it.

C.S. Lewis illustrates this in his Chronicles of Narnia book titled *The Magician's Nephew*. Late in the story, the main antagonist, Uncle Andrew, finds himself in Narnia by magic. He witnesses Aslan, the Jesus figure and protagonist, speaking Narnia into being through song. But there is a problem. Aslan presents himself as a huge lion. And because of Uncle Andrew's hard heart and preconceptions, he is unable to hear Aslan's song. He hears only a lion roaring. The children in the story, Digory and Jill, ask Aslan to help Uncle Andrew. But, as Aslan explains, there is nothing he can do to help someone who doesn't want help.

> *This world is bursting with life for these few days because the song with which I called it into life still hangs in the air and rumbles in the ground. It will not be so for long. But I cannot tell that to this old sinner, and I cannot comfort him either; he has made himself unable to hear my voice. If I spoke to him, he would hear only growlings and roarings. Oh, Adam's sons, how cleverly you defend yourselves against all that might do you good!* [102]

Did you get this—"*he has made himself unable to hear my voice*"? It is not that Aslan cannot be heard. The issue is that Uncle Andrew has made himself unable to hear.

The redemption of the Lord Jesus Christ on the cross is fully available, accomplished, and effective for all humanity. But, for us to experience the fruit of that redemption, we must accept it. Even for those of us who have accepted the redemption of our sin, there is more available. This is also true of our stories.

My heart breaks when I see Christians struggling with

shame and guilt because they won't allow Jesus to redeem their stories. Too often, we "accept Christ" but don't really understand the fullness of the freedom available through the work of Christ on our behalf.

The redemption of both our story and our gifting is fundamental to the creation of the tov heart within us. Our ability to live the abundant life Jesus promised.

But too often, our unwillingness to release our story to Jesus for redemption prevents us from being everything God intended.

> *Our lives have often been painful, yes? So, we think life is full of scarcity and not abundance. But then there are those times when, out of nowhere, somehow, the world expresses its longing to be whole. And suddenly, God steps in. And we are pulled out of our blindness, and we're invited into redemption. I know I was. I know you were.*[103]

The stories of addiction, abuse, and trauma that either we committed or came against us. The things we said or didn't say but should have. The resulting regret, fear, anger, shame, guilt, and ambivalence. All these keep us in bondage. Bound in our grave clothes. Unable to live our lives with integrity and in truth.

Remember, it is the man who has nothing to hide, nothing to fear, and nothing to prove who can fulfill his true purpose and create environments where life can flourish.

Pause for a few minutes to ask Jesus, "*Is there any part of my story that I have not given to you for redemption? Held back and hidden?*" Listen. Wait. Persist with the question. Wait.

Jesus, I give you my story. Every nuance and whisper. Every word and action. Every thought and interpretation. Every reaction and response. I allow your work on the cross to wash over me, to cleanse me, to renew me. I give you permission to storm the beaches of my heart to heal my broken stories and set me free.[104] *Amen!*

YOUR STORY REDEEMED

"*For God is not merely mending, not simply restoring a status quo. Redeemed humanity is to be something more glorious than unfallen humanity.*" – C.S. Lewis

TOV MARKER

What has gone before has been orientation. The redemption of your story is where the journey of your heart into tov begins. A journey requiring some farming. Through the redemption of your story Jesus wants to set you free. But you must participate. You must accept and live out of that freedom. Leaving behind shame, guilt, and fear. Leaving behind pride, arrogance, and resentment. We were all something else before we met Jesus. In and through the redemption of your story, when others see and experience it, they can also be set free. This is the beauty and power of your story redeemed. The beauty and power of tov!

It is through your redeemed story that your heart becomes tov. And for your heart to become tov, you must do some farming. Only through the farming of your story will your heart become the fertile ground necessary to live the abundant life.

I won't lie—farming your story can be hard work, and as with all hard work in our lives, process is involved. The process is not strict ABC, but it is process, nonetheless. And, as we learned earlier, process takes time and cannot be compromised, bypassed, or shortcut.

Three parameters govern all processes: time, cost, and quality. The biggest problem we have is that we can only choose two of those parameters to affect the outcome. The phrase used in the project management world is, "Time, cost, and quality—pick two."

If you want something fast at a low cost, it won't be good. If you want something high quality at a low cost, it will take time. If you want something quick and high quality, it will cost you.

If you are willing to put in the time and, as Jesus put it, count the cost,[105] you will reap the reward. Producing an abundant, quality crop as Jesus promised. But if you rush the process or are not willing to "count the cost," the outcome will not be what either you or God desires. Remember Yvon Chenard's warning; if you compromise the process, you will end up back where you started.

Two initial insights are critical to the process of farming your tov heart, the tov heart within you.

The first is that you need to know your story. The second is that you must let Jesus redeem it.

Most of us don't think much about our stories. We have "moved on" from how we grew up, who our friends were, and what our family was like. And we certainly don't give much consideration to our successes and failures as we stepped into adulthood.

If we're honest with ourselves, if our story was "good," we turned it into either pride or humor. If our story was "bad," we either turned it into blame and resentment or we stuffed it. The good showing up as either arrogance or self-diminishment. And the bad becoming either victimhood or denial.

But Jesus wants more. He wants to set your heart free to be all he created you to be. He wants your story redeemed!

It is for freedom that Christ set you free. – Galatians 5:1

Jesus wants you to live out of a heart set free from pride and arrogance. From shame, fear, and guilt. A heart lived with integrity and in truth. Where you are able and willing to acknowledge and own who you were, who you are, and lean with expectancy into who you are becoming. All without contempt or pride.

If you are to recover your tov heart, you must take part by first acknowledging and knowing your story. Not reliving the pain, trauma, joy, or success to rehash them. But to invite Jesus into your story so healing, renewal, and redemption can take place.

Your story is redeemed by the blood of the Lord Jesus Christ shed on the cross. He has ransomed you. Everything you have done, everything done to you, was paid for to set you free from the consequences of your story.

> *"For he has rescued us from the dominion of darkness and brought us into the kingdom of the Son he loves, in whom we have redemption, the forgiveness of sins."*
> – Colossians 1:13-14

Notice that Paul says, *"the forgiveness of sins"*. He doesn't say *"the forgiveness of your sins"* but *"the forgiveness of sins."* Your sins and the sins of others against you and the ones you love can be redeemed. But first you must trust, in both your head and your heart, that Jesus' work of redemption is true and accomplished.

You know your story is redeemed when you can sit with it in truth. Holding everything loosely as you acknowledge, *"That is what I experienced and who I was. That's not who I am."*

Remember the great conversation between Phillip and Matthew from the TV series *The Chosen* I spoke of earlier. Matthew is struggling with his story as a tax collector, a betrayer of his people who chose prosperity over his family, friends, and others. Even after choosing to follow Jesus, there are those who continually remind him of his past. Just like there are those who continually remind you of who you used to be. Who he *was*. Who you *were*. Phillip offers Matthew another perspective, a way to look at his story differently.

> *"I 'was' something else once too. Once you've met the Messiah, 'am' is all that matters."*[106]

Paul puts it this way:

> *"Therefore, if anyone is in Christ, the new creation has come;*

the old has gone, the new has come!"
– 2 Corinthians 5:17 NIV 1984

You are not who you were. Your past does dictate or define your present or your future. Unless you let it.

Don't get me wrong, the process is not about forgetting or losing who you were. Who you were is important, because it is in and through your story that you connect with others. It is in and through your story, known and shared fully and honestly, that you connect with and help others find the freedom Jesus wants for them. Exactly like he wants for you.

One of the biggest problems in the church is the uncorrected assumption by new believers that those they see in the church are different from them. That they don't have a past and that who they are now is who they have always been. They have no idea that they used to be something else too.

This assumption breeds diminishment, isolation, fear, and an unspoken sense of rejection. We all were *"something else"* before we met Jesus. Now, because of Jesus, we are different!

But I want to offer a word of caution here. In this process, I guarantee you, your story will be mishandled. You may be shunned, ostracized, misunderstood, and criticized. But don't be afraid, be discerning. Discerning how, where, and with whom you share your unvarnished truth. Ask Jesus how much and how deeply to share, and with whom, especially at first.

But, when you can share your story with anyone, anywhere, with integrity and in truth, as God calls you to share it, your story has been redeemed. Nothing to hide, nothing to fear, and nothing to prove.

> *"Always be prepared to give an answer to everyone who asks you to give the reason for the hope that you have. But do this with gentleness and respect, keeping a clear conscience, so that those who speak maliciously against your good behavior in Christ may be ashamed of their slander."* – 1 Peter 3:15–16

As a follower of Christ, you can author the remaining chapters of your story with Jesus. To do that, you must know and be able to honestly share your true past with others. You must be able to share your redeemed story with integrity and in truth. Without shame, guilt, and fear.

If you allow Jesus to redeem your story, he will remove the shame, guilt, and fear. And as you walk with him in that freedom, you will be able to show those around you that they can trust him. And so, in turn, they can do the same. First for themselves, and then for others around them in ever-widening ripples of redemption. A harvest one hundred, sixty, or thirty times what was sown.

This is the beauty and power of your story redeemed!

> *Our lives have often been painful, yes? So, we think life is full of scarcity and not abundance. But then there are those times when, out of nowhere, somehow, the world expresses its longing to be whole. And suddenly, God steps in. And we are pulled out of our blindness, and we're invited into redemption. I know I was. I know you were.*[107]

YOU ARE GIFTED

"...for God's gifts and his call are irrevocable." – Romans 11:29

"We have different gifts, according to the grace given to each of us..." – Romans 12:6a

TOV MARKER

You are imparted by God with unique talents and abilities. These gifts are often the things you do easily and naturally without effort or thought. But your gifts have been opposed and diminished. Leaning into God and the counsel of trusted friends helps you to recognize and embrace them.

Have you ever taken one of those spiritual gift assessments? You know, the ones that tell you you'll find your place of service in the church. Hospitality equals the Greeting or Food Prep Team. Teaching equals Small Group Leader or Children/Youth Ministry. And administration equals serving on the Church Audit Committee. Don't get me wrong, these are good things. But just because they are being done in a church context does not necessarily make them God things.

The gifts I am talking about here are the talents and abilities imparted to you by God. Your unique ability to focus. Your special heart of compassion. Your ability to see others when most don't. Your ability to easily converse with strangers. Or, your ability to problem-solve or mediate. Your gifts may be physical, mental, emotional, or, most likely, a combination of all three in varying measure.

Your gifts are most simply defined as those things you can do easily and almost without thought or exertion. And, while the categories of our gifting may be generic, that gifting is expressed in the world uniquely, in the divine context of your creation and your story. The singular expression of diplomacy, painting, teaching, animal husbandry, hospitality, or, the sciences.

> **Your creation** – *You are uniquely created reflecting the image God, fearfully and wonderfully made.*[108]

> **Your story** – *No one else has seen and experienced the world as you have.*

Digest that for a minute. If it were not true, everyone with the same gift would be a clone, the exact same expression of the same gift. It would be true for any gift you can think of. Without the unique expression of gifts within the context of our unique humanity, those with similar gifts would present them to the world in exactly the same way.

Yet, we know from practical experience that not all painters paint the same way or the same thing. And even if they were all asked to paint the same tree, those paintings would be as unique and diverse and expressed in as many ways as there are painters.

Interestingly, the same is true technologically. Take software for example. While there are structures and syntax within a programming language, the expression of that language is unique and dependent upon the programmer. And as programs become more complex, they also become more and more unique.

This is also true of our gifting. The more complex our stories, the more uniquely our gifting is expressed in the world. Unfortunately, for most of us our gifts are hidden in plain sight, and we often fail to recognize them and live out their full expression in our lives. Or, they have mutated to become weapons of self-protection.

In many cases our gifting usually comes to us so easily that we believe "*anyone could do it.*" The ease with which our gifting flows in and through us becomes an obstacle to recognizing and stepping into it. We come to believe everyone can do what we can do. So, we minimize our gifting's expression in our lives and thus our affect in and our effect on the world.

For others, their gifting has become weaponized. A tool used to support the poser and self-protect. A means to elevate them above others to ensure their identity is safe or to ensure they are protected from physical, emotional, or mental assault.

Your gifting is also where you receive some of your most devastating wounds. The arrows and the body blows you experience within the context of your story are most often aimed at your gifting. The Evil One's goal here is the same as it is in all his work. Separation.

The Enemy knows how powerful your redeemed story is when connected to your redeemed gifting. Even as you walk with Jesus in the redemption of your story, if the enemy can separate you from your gifting, your glory, the impact that God intended when he created you, is diminished, may even be extinguished.

THE TOV HEART

YOUR GIFTING REDEEMED

"We are all gifted. That is our inheritance." – Ethel Waters

TOV MARKER
Your gifting is the portion of God's Glory imparted to you and that he intends to impact the world through. It is here, in your gifting, that you often take the biggest hits. Unfortunately, most of us don't recognize our gifting or have used it as a club or diminished it. As you lean into God for the redemption of your gifting, it is important to find balance – to see yourself truly. No more AND no less than God created you to be.

We think of humility as putting others before yourself, and rightly so.

> *"Do nothing out of selfish ambition or vain conceit. But in humility consider others above yourselves. Each of you should look not only to your own interests, but also to the interests of the others."*
> – Philippians 2:3-4 NIV 1984

But we also need to be careful. Humility does not, at the same time, diminish who God created you to be. Too often in the church, to protect against the sin of pride,[109] this verse is used to diminish our own gifting. But there must be balance.
Jesus himself, the perfection of humility, never stopped

being God, creator of all that is. And, in his humility never stopped displaying that to those around him. In his perfected humility he was still God.[110]

You take some of your greatest wounds in the realm of your gifting. The enemy knows who you are. He knows that through your story and gifting God imparted to you a portion of his own Glory. A glory God intends to release into the world.

> *"The story of your life is the story of the long and brutal assault on your heart by the one who knows what you could be and fears it."*[111]

Why does the enemy fear you so? First, because of your story. It is in the details of your story and your ability to share it without fear that you connect with the hearts of others. Second, because of your gifting. The way God has imparted himself in you. Allowing you to uniquely connect with others in a way no other person in the world can.

Your gifting may be a winsome spirit, a compassionate heart, some technical or athletic ability, or ease with art or music. There are as many giftings as there are people uniquely created to bear them. Each gift is a small embodiment of a portion of the Glory of God. That is why you most often take your greatest wounds in your gifting. It is the evidence of the Glory of God placed within you that the Evil One wishes to extinguish.

But God intends to use your unique combination of story and gifting to impact the world. And both must be redeemed for them to bear the fruit God intends.

How do you know what your gifting is? That is a journey for you and God to take together.

Ask Yourself: What do you do easily and without effort? So often it is the things we easily do that are the easiest for us to ignore and for the Evil One to diminish. It may be that early in our lives, our gifting was abused or rejected by our family. A gifting for sports opposed by our artist parents or a gifting for art or music opposed by a parent who wanted a pro ball player.

What is it that you do easily and without effort? Take this seriously, no matter how "small" it may seem. Write it down.

Ask Others: Bring to your closest friends or family the simple questions, "*Why do you want to be with me?*" and "*What about me draws you to me?*" Not asking those simple questions can prevent us from seeing the gifting God has endowed us with. I guarantee that those closest to you see it, feel it, and experience it. Be careful here to only ask those you trust to tell you the truth. The Evil One can use and has used others in your life to shut down, twist, and diminish your gifting. Be a bit cautious here. Again, write the answers down.

Ask God: Depending where you are on your journey with God, it may be harder to hear his voice or trust that you are hearing him correctly.

Take your two lists, the one you made for yourself and the one you received from others and merge them. Take special notice of gifts that are the same or similar on both lists.

Now bring your list to God. "*Lord, I give these gifts to you for redemption and healing. I ask for your interpretation and understanding. Is there anything that is missing, Lord? Bring these gifts to life in me; to the glory you created in me before the foundation of the world.*"

"How blessed is God! And what a blessing he is! He's the Father of our Master, Jesus Christ, and takes us to the high places of blessing in him. Long before he laid down earth's foundations, he had us in mind, had settled on us as the focus of his love, to be made whole and holy by his love." – Ephesians 1:3-6 MSG

Take your time. This is not a race. Sit with this question for days or weeks if necessary. And when you recognize them, write them down. Accept them as true, and that your expression of them in the world is singular and unique. Then consecrate them!

Jesus, I bring your Kingdom, your Life, your Love, and your Glory over, in, and through the gifting you have given me. I accept my gifts and thank you for them. I release my gifting to you, Lord Jesus, for your provision and protection. Redeem my gifting, Lord, that I may become all you created me to be! Amen!

Lastly, hold your gifting in *Balance*. As you lean into the truth of the gifting God has given you, you will be pulled in one or two directions by the Evil One in concert with your own sin nature. The first may be toward pride and arrogance. The second is back toward diminishment.

In pride and arrogance, your gifting, either consciously or unconsciously, is used as a club to get your way in the world. You step on hearts and destroy lives to get your own way and ensure you are ... successful, happy, wealthy, etc.

In diminishment, your gifting is minimized and hidden. Showing itself in some form of the statement, "*I have nothing special to offer anyone.*"

To protect against both attacks, acknowledge your gifts before God and thank him for them. And, at the same time, rejoice that others around you are also gifted in their own unique ways. Don't diminish someone else's gifting and don't allow someone else's gifting to diminish your own.

Praise God's intention to impact the world through the fullness and completeness of his Church, united and one in and through union with Jesus.[112]

There is an instructive and beautiful song in the animated movie, *The Prince of Egypt*,[113] called "Through Heaven's Eyes."[114]

> *So how can you see what your life is worth*
> *Or where your value lies?*
> *You can never see through the eyes of man*
> *You must look at your life*
> *Look at your life through heaven's eyes*

The entire song is worth both a listen and a read of the lyrics.

Balance is the key to holding your gifting with integrity and truth. Balance is the humility of who God created you to be. No more AND no less.

LOVE REVISITED

> "*A new command I give you: Love one another. As I have loved you, so you must love one another. By this everyone will know that you are my disciples, if you love one another.*" – John 13:24-35

TOV MARKER

We often hide behind our screens. Subtly, we become who and what we don't want to be. Like the rest of the world, we fall into the Evil One's snare. The result being that the fruit we share with the world is not the love Jesus told us to share.

I used to spend a lot of time and energy on Facebook. Politics and social issues would get me riled up. What started out as a brief "conversation" rapidly descended into argument. And, sometimes, fueled by anger and frustration, turned into a diatribe. I would spend hours researching statistics, thinking of clever retorts, and honing the point of my rhetorical rapier.

Then Jesus showed up. He showed me that all my effort, anger, and frustration only resulted in the diminishment of my "foe" in my heart. Resulting in the deterioration of my ability to love. This was especially true when my "opponent" was another Christian. When I was too lazy or too agitated to write from my own heart, I would take something that had come into my "feed." Something someone else had written. Someone I usually didn't know but that spoke to what I was feeling and had the right jab and oomph. I would pass that along without thought or comment. Thereby proclaiming, "This is what I believe."

I admit at times it felt good. That hard-hitting meme, that cutting intellectual retort, or that stinging sarcastic remark. Yet it stoked in me a smoldering fire of hatred and malice toward others. Toward "friends," some of whom I knew well and many I didn't.

Jesus gives us clear guidance here. He calls us to more.

> *You will recognize them by their fruits. Are grapes gathered from thornbushes, or figs from thistles? So, every healthy tree bears good fruit, but the diseased tree bears bad fruit. A healthy tree cannot bear bad fruit, nor can a diseased tree bear good fruit. Every tree that does not bear good fruit is cut down and thrown into the fire. Thus, you will recognize them by their fruits.*
> – Matthew 7:16-20 ESV

Yes, he was speaking here specifically about false prophets, but his words are true in all situations as a general principle. You will know them by their fruit. And the fruit of my actions was anger and frustration, diminishment and dismissal. The opposite of the love, compassion, and grace Jesus calls us to. And this was especially true when it came to fellow Christians, he called me to love.

For me, the Holy Spirit works as I sleep. I go to bed one way and wake up another. And as usually happens when God gets hold of my heart, I change. In this case, I pulled the ejection handle and left Facebook.

Don't get me wrong, there can be benefits to Facebook. Connection with old friends and family. Pictures of children and grandchildren from across the country. Shared joy in the joy of others. Shared compassion in the pain of those close to us.

That's how it begins. But then we see pain and trauma close to us. Then in the lives of our friends' friends, their friends, our neighborhood and state, our country, and lastly, the world. By then, we're wasted, emaciated, frustrated, and angry. There is just too much craziness out there in this broken world for our hearts to hold it all. Too much was tugging at my good heart, and I became hard, emotionally and spiritually. We were not meant to hold the trauma of the world in our hearts. It's deadly to our relationships with others and Jesus to attempt to do so. Over time, it kills our ability to truly love.

That doesn't mean we turn a blind eye to the pain and trauma or that we refuse to care. Just the opposite. We release those things to the one who can effect change, restore hearts and lives, and heal, renew, and redeem. My friend David told me years ago, *"We don't have to have all the answers, because we know the one who does."* We release these things to God. Not out of apathy, complacency, or ambivalence but in love. Because we know the one who can hold each one, personally and intimately. The one who can and will move mountains!

I understand that many people, especially younger generations, are no longer on Facebook. But the same is true for Instagram, X, and TikTok. All social media is ripe for the invasion of the work of the Evil One and its effect on our hearts and minds. Hatred, malice, anxiety, frustration, and fear. Unfortunately, if we are not vigilant, it doesn't take much to give him a foothold in our lives.

> *"In your anger do not sin: Do not let the sun go down while you are still angry, and do not give the devil a foothold."*
> – Ephesians 4:26-27

Or as the ESV puts it,

> *"Be angry and do not sin; do not let the sun go down on your anger and give no opportunity to the devil."*

Paul's example here is anger. But footholds or opportunities, if you will, are not only established through anger. Anger is a readily accessible entry point for the Evil One because of the theft, death, and destruction in the world.[115] Anger very easily goes from *"What is being done is wrong"* to *"The person doing the wrong thing is evil."*

From there, it becomes easy to lump people together into an evil mob of racists, drunkards, addicts, or homophobes. *"Pick your poison"* is how the old saying goes, and poison it is. It will kill you in the end as surely as if you broke a cyanide capsule between your teeth. It will kill your relationships, even with those closest to you. It will kill your heart. And in the name of "love," it will kill your ability to love.

Sadly, I see professing Christians aligning their hearts and minds with hatred, malice, diminishment, rage, and anger on social media. Demonstrating the fruit of the Evil

One's hold on their hearts. The fruit of the Spirit being nowhere to be found.

It breaks my heart to see people who, face to face, appear to be sincere and genuine in their love for Jesus and his work in their lives. But, when "hidden" behind their screen, display the worst that their broken hearts can profess to the world. Whether it's their own words or the words of others, it becomes a demonstration to the world that there is no salt and no light. Just angry bullies or timid bystanders. I have been the latter for much too long.

> *"Boldness apart from brokenness makes a bully. Brokenness apart from boldness makes a bystander." – David Benham*

For that, I repent. I change, turn, and am different.

Brothers and sisters! Think about what the one who died on the cross and shed his blood for your abominations told us,

> *"By this everyone will know that you are my disciples, if you love one another." –* John 13:35

> *"Every tree that does not bear good fruit is cut down and thrown into the fire. Thus, you will recognize them by their fruits."*
> – Matthew 7:19

You are not hidden. You are known. You are seen.

> *The student is not above the teacher, nor a servant above his master. It is enough for students to be like their teachers, and servants like their masters. If the head of the house has been called*

> *Beelzebul, how much more the members of his household! So do not be afraid of them, for there is nothing concealed that will not be disclosed, or hidden that will not be made known. What I tell you in the dark, speak in the daylight; what is whispered in your ear, proclaim from the roofs. Do not be afraid of those who kill the body but cannot kill the soul. Rather, be afraid of the One who can destroy both soul and body in hell.*
> – Matthew 10:24-28

Brothers, what fruit is your tree bearing to the world? What is the fruit that wells up in your heart and expresses itself online? Is it fruit that wells up to eternal life? Or is it a poisoned apple? It cannot be both. You will be known by your fruit.

> *"All your life you've been asleep. Make straight the way of the King. He is here to awaken the earth. But some will not want to waken. They are in love with the dark. I wonder which one you'll be?"*
> – John the Baptist to Nicodemus, *The Chosen*[116]

YOUR GLORY, YOUR IMPACT

"For the glory of God is the living man" – St. Irenaeus[117]

TOV MARKER

It is through the redemption of your story and gifting, set in the context of God's love, that the world experiences the impact God intended you to bring to the world. This is the fruit of God Math. The way through which you are able to create environments that flourish. Live abundantly - tov.

Your redeemed story plus your redeemed gifting, in the context of God's love, is the glory he intends to impact the world with through you.

Together, in the context of God's love, your redeemed story and gifting become the beautiful, unique glory God meant when he created you. The glory he will use, if we have the courage to let him, to impact the lives of those around us. To join with Jesus in the process of creation and recreation of your tov heart. To create environments where life can flourish.

As I said before, it takes some farming. Beautiful, hard, consistent farming. The farming of your story and your gifting, in the context of God's love, to create in you the tov heart from which you can live abundantly.

In and through your tov heart you create environments around you where life can flourish. The abundant life Jesus promised you. Shared with others.

A few years ago, *Wild at Heart* organized an unstructured program called FIRES. It was based on a literal shared dream of several saints. A dream where, looking down on the globe of the world, they saw fires starting to light up. A few at first, then more and more until the globe was covered in fires.

In Scripture, the Holy Spirit is often spoken of in terms of fire.

> *"For the Lord your God is a consuming fire."*
> – Deuteronomy 4:24

> *"They saw what seemed to be tongues of fire that separated and came to rest on each of them. All of them were filled with the Holy Spirit..."* – Acts 2:3-4

These fires are born out of God's work in the lives of his people. His work to redeem stories and gifting. And, in the context of his great love, they are released into the world as the glory he intends to impact the world with. Through you.

Your tov heart and the abundant life Jesus promised. Life that starts as a spark, turns into a flame, and burns brightly in the world. Cleansing and offering light, love, and, ultimately, more tov.

WHAT ALREADY IS

"And no one puts new wine into old wineskins. For the old skins would burst from the pressure, spilling the wine and ruining the skins. New wine is stored in new wineskins so that both are preserved."
– Matthew 9:17 NLT

TOV MARKER

Do not let yourself become discouraged. You are already on your way to tov and the abundant life. Yes, there is more road to travel and process to experience but recognize and embrace what already is. Thank God for it, step into it, and continue the journey to becoming who God created you to be.

I love the way Jesus puts pieces together using both the old and the new.

Not long ago, Jesus asked me to renew my understanding of his work. His cross, resurrection, and ascension. Years ago, *Wild at Heart*[118] released a great resource called *"The Work of Christ."*[119] I dug it out of my CD vault. Pause. Yes, I still have CDs. For those of you born after the mid-nineties, CDs are those small, shiny disks that look like DVD/Blu-ray discs but only contain audio. Yep, I'm a boomer.

Anyway, I pulled out the CDs to refresh my memory of what is objectively true of the Gospel. I had listened to them before but, as often happens when we engage the Gospel, this time was a bit different. It was a deeper dive into what he has done. I found myself rejoicing and thanking Jesus from the depths of my heart and soul for his great work of love and life!

Maybe it was a deeper awareness of my own sin or the war against my heart. Or, a greater appreciation for his great work of love and fierceness that had set me free. Most likely, it was a mix of all the above, in unique measure to my need. God does that!

Whatever it was, as I listened to each session, Jesus took me deeper until I got to the ascension, and John said,

> *Okay, our destiny is to rule. That's our human destiny. Let's go back to that now. Genesis 1. We're created to rule. It's just written into the fabric of our being. And you experience it in hundreds of ways in your life. Any time you ever want to make things better. Anywhere. In anything, right? I want to clean the house, that's ruling, right? Want to plant a garden, that's ruling. Want to send a letter to a friend to encourage them. Any time you want to make things better by your presence, you bring something of yourself to bear on a situation to make it better, that's Adam and Eve. That's what you're designed to do. And we love to do it in ways that are unique to us. Some people want to build, some people want to speak, some people want to touch, right, to minister, and other people want to sing, befriend. I mean, it's as diverse as human personality. But the destiny is to rule. We are created to do that.*

Immediately, the Spirit of God made a connection ... our glory can be as simple as a hug!

In my small group at a previous church, there was a woman whose glory is a hug. That is how she rules. No matter who, no matter what, no matter where, a hug from her is better than gold!

Then God asked me to look in the mirror, and the knowing moved completely from my head to my heart. He took me into my own glory, new and fresh, what already is, in the context of what has always been objectively true. Old wine in old wineskins. Maturing and becoming better with age. Such a blessing!

Today, I was listening to a podcast on ambivalence about the return of Jesus. I was intrigued by a woman who doesn't want Jesus to come back yet because there is so much in her life that she hasn't experienced. As I connected and related to her story, the pieces fell into place in my own life. New wine in new wineskins.

I desire to do more to affect the hearts of people by helping them recognize, lean into, and live out of the glory God has created in them. Part of me desires a "big ministry impact" on the world. I want to write, and I want to see people set free to live from their glory and not from their fear. I want. I want. I want.

But I have come to realize and accept that if it is only one, it is enough. If God put me on this earth so that one other person's heart becomes tov and they live abundant life, that is enough. I hope it is more, but one is enough.[120]

> *"It's not what He isn't giving but what He is giving. We can get so locked onto what we don't have, what we think we want or need, that we miss the gifts that God is giving."*[121]

But the more I think about it, it isn't only what he is giving that we miss, but it is also what he has already given. We miss the glory he has already created in us. The glory lived out in the day-to-day interactions of our lives. The glory that most of us have worked hard to hide and shut down because we have found it to be misunderstood, opposed, and, quite frankly, problematic.

We stifle our own glory! Yes, in part because it is opposed. But mainly because the "World" has taught us, through its assault and the resulting wounds, that when we live out of our glory, it is painful. We are misunderstood, shamed, and abused. The Evil One takes our glory and merges it with our wounds. Then, when we try to live out of our glory, the result is that we live it out in pride or arrogance or neediness.

Even when we get a glimpse of the true glory God has created in us, we are so close to it that we can't see it for what it is. How we have been called to rule. We take our glory for granted, *"That's nothing special."* We dismiss it, *"Everyone can do that."* So, we stifle the thousands of little ways we proclaim the coming of the Kingdom of God through the glory he has created in us. And, we remain hidden.

Yet that is how we rule! We rule not in the "big impact" or who we will become, but in who we *already are*, here and now. We miss it. I missed it.

But, oh! When you recognize the glory God has created in you, lean into it, and have the courage to release it into the world. Without fear, shame, or guilt. That is when you truly step into the authority of Christ and rule in your kingdom. That is when you become a part of the Kingdom of God.

Not someday when you rule in the Kingdom when Jesus comes again, but *now*! Not "Someday." What you dream of or aspire toward. Not in the future of what "could be," but in the actual here and now! The true glory he created in each of us from the beginning of the world! Therein lies the cure for, at least, some of the ambivalence that keeps us from longing for Christ's return with our whole hearts. You, me, and all the saints, stepping into the fullness and completion of what already is. As we continue to become who God created us to be!

> *"The most important thing in your life is not what you do. It is who you become."* – Dallas Willard[122]

CHAPTER 9

FARMING TOV

*"Human flourishing is the outcome of the
redemptive work of Jesus Christ
in any person's life."*
JOHN ELDREDGE

BUSHWACKING

> **Jim:** *"The whole section is closed off. Something's wrong."*
>
> **Aurora:** *"We're looking for wrong."*[123]

TOV MARKER

Farming begins with bushwacking and the easiest way to bushwack is to identify what's wrong. As you proceed, it is important to walk with Jesus for context and interpretation. And, as you begin to find freedom, remember that clarity is not healing. The process will be hard and sometimes painful but the freedom and life available is unimaginable. Don't give up. You're just getting started.

The process of farming begins with bushwacking. Bushwacking means to clear a path through dense vegetation. Physically cutting them down with a hatchet, machete or similar tool. It is the preparation of an area for planting by removing unwanted brush, thick bushes, and small scrub trees.

If we are to be who God created us to be, to find the tov heart and live abundantly, we must start by clearing the brush that has grown up in and over our hearts.

The easiest way to do this is by looking for what is wrong. What has been broken, lost, obstructed, forgotten, or diminished.

We know something's wrong. It's been wrong for a very long time. Ever since Adam and Eve mistrusted the goodness of God in the Garden.

As a result, everyone's life has overgrowth. The dense vegetation that has grown up in and around our hearts. Sealing them up and closing them off.

Too often we don't recognize it as wrong. It's the way we react to adversity and joy. The way we interact with others. Our "way" has become so much a part of us that we have come to believe that this is just who we are.

The brush of our hearts is the result of our actions and reactions to life. The nuanced wisecracks and jibes of friends and family. The physical or mental abuse we experienced as children and young adults. The subtle lessons through which we learned to navigate our home and school culture. Along with the many ways we learned to achieve validation and approval.

Pause for a moment. Take out pen and paper and consider this question: "*What are the things you believe you are not?*"

I am not comfortable in crowds.
I am not good at art or sports.
I can't do math.
I can't get up on stage.
I'm not good at talking to people.
I can't. I'm not.

Take your list and ask yourself the next question. "*Why do I think that?*" It's always good to ask the next question. The next question always takes us deeper, especially if we invite Jesus into it.

> *"Jesus, why do I think that?"*
> *"Jesus, how many of these things are not "I can't" but are really "I don't think I can?"*

Some of these things you may not be able to do for valid reasons. For example, you will never play pro basketball because you're five foot five inches tall. But I guarantee you that many of them, especially the relational ones, are doable.

As you listen to Jesus, cross out the ones that are valid and rewrite your list of the questionable "can'ts." The things that you believe you can't do or aren't capable of doing "simply because." This is the list you take back to Jesus and your closest friends and ask, *"Are these really true?"* This process, over time, will begin to cut down the brush in and around your heart.

Because our stories have been and continue to be lived in a world at war (more on that later), we have all taken hits. Some whizzed by and missed us but were close enough that we took notice. Others grazed us and made us wary and afraid. Still others hit us mid-chest, right in the heart. And so, we let the brush grow, and the weeds and the thicket of thorns that keep others from getting too close. The fear and anxiety, the doubt and confusion, the arrogance and pride, the anger and rage. Whatever form your brush takes, it ensures that your heart is protected from others. And that you are only seen as the world wants to see you.

As you begin bushwhacking, this is brush you must cut down. The brush you've let grow up over a lifetime of shame, guilt, and pain to protect your heart from yourself and others.

Shame, guilt, and pain come in various forms and in many ways and always results in fear. Fear is the motivation behind most of the evil in the world, and fear is behind all separation. Separation from God and others. The goal of the Evil One and his work in our lives.

Bushwhacking, when done in partnership with Jesus, allows us to identify the brush that has led to separation. And once identified, we can begin to remove it. But bushwhacking is usually pretty painful. Not only does it entail cutting down the brush, but we must also dig out the roots. The roots have wrapped themselves so tightly around our hearts that the bushwhacking can feel like it is killing us. These roots have grown so deep and spread so broadly that the pain, at times, may seem unbearable.

One of my largest weeds was the absence of my father. But unlike those whose fathers may have ignored or beaten them, mine was non-existent. From a "father" perspective, I lived as an orphan.

My parents divorced when I was three, and my father left and never came back. I never knew him. Growing up, I would see other dads in the park or at sporting events with their kids, and to protect my heart, I would tell myself it didn't matter. *Never had him, don't miss him.* Over the course of my life, that brush grew tree-size. The roots went down deep into my heart and spread through my life, manifesting themselves in a sense of absolute self-reliance as a way to self-protect. I didn't need anyone—not my mother, not my godfather, not my uncles. I had it all under control and didn't need help, counsel, or support. It was a small seed planted when I was three years old. For over fifty years it grew until its roots wrapped tightly around my heart and extended broadly throughout every area of my life.

Even after much work and the intellectual acknowledgment of the loss, it was over 15 years from the start of my restoration journey with Jesus before it moved from my head to my heart. The beginning of freedom.

It was the last night of a lay counseling program. My peers had called me out for "bullshitting" my way through a session. It was then that God and I began to dig out the roots of my loss. I had previously cut down the brush, but the roots still lived. It was horribly painful, and it was absolutely liberating. I literally cried for three hours.

Previously I had intellectually assented to my never having a father as an issue. I had understood it in my head. But it was then that the reality moved from my head to my heart. I had never grieved the loss of my father. That night I did. And it set me free!

John Eldredge puts it this way, "*Clarity is not healing.*"

Bushwhacking is some of the hardest work you will ever do. You may initially find it enlightening and illuminating. Identifying and seeing the brush in our lives is pretty self-satisfying. But please, please remember clarity is *not* healing. Understanding is not restoration.

Clarity provides focus and direction, the ability to see the large obstacles so that they can be cut down. But to be set free, you must continue to dig down deep to remove the roots as you prepare the soil of your heart for planting.

I won't sugarcoat it. Bushwhacking is hard. It is painful. It is embarrassing and can leave us with holes in our "poser" identity. Yet bushwacking is also refreshing and freeing. The deeper we dig, the more barriers to relationship and freedom we remove. We begin to recognize and address the places in our lives we have used to self-protect. The places the Evil One has used as footholds. To "steal, kill, and destroy." To separate us from God and from others.

No matter how hard it gets, and it will get hard, don't give up. It will be harder than you thought possible. But as you enter this work with Jesus, the freedom on the other side is more glorious than you could dream or imagine. I like how *The Message* phrases Paul's words in Ephesians 3:20.

> *"God can do anything, you know—far more than you could ever imagine or guess or request in your wildest dreams! He does it not by pushing us around but by working within us, his Spirit deeply and gently within us."*

Now for a warning. There is a lot of freedom that comes from bushwacking. Don't let that be enough for you. If you truly want the tov heart and the abundance Jesus promised, there is more work to do. Remember, farming is hard work and takes time.

PLOWING

"Do not make light of a fall even if it be the most venial of faults; rather, be quick to repair it by repentance." – Saint Basil

TOV MARKER

Plowing breaks up the dense, crusty soil of our hearts. Our sin and the sin of others, into smaller chunks, exposing it to light and air. This brings nutrients to the surface and ushers in forgiveness and love through the work of Christ deep within our hearts.

The farming process continues with plowing. Soil left untended becomes hard and dense. Plowing is the next step toward tov and abundance. Plowing opens the earth up. Breaking dense, crusty soil into smaller chunks, exposing it to air and light. Plowing also turns over the uppermost layer of soil. Bringing fresh nutrients to the surface. Burying any leftover weeds and residue to decay so they will not affect new plant growth.

After we have worked with God in the hard labor of bushwhacking, we must now begin to tend the soil of our heart.

We are opposed by three grand forces which we will look closer at later—The World, The Flesh, and The Devil. But as we cut down and dig out the obstructions that have kept us from stepping into all that God has called us to be. That have separated us from God and others. We must deal with the hard, crusty soil of the flesh—sin.

Sin takes two primary forms in our lives. The sin we commit and the sin of others against us. Most often the two are intertwined. We sin, and that sin affects others. Others sin, and that sin affects us. Either way the effect of third-party sin on us or on others leads to ancillary sin in our own lives. Reaction directs the story. We react badly or others react badly, and the sin cycle spirals out of control. Sometimes, these sins may be very subtle. A passing thought or a whispered comment. From the unjust taking of a human life to a middle finger on the freeway, sin in all its forms and expressions hardens our hearts.

So, what is the antidote to sin? Repentance, the blood of Christ, and love. You have heard this before, but because we are such forgetful creatures, I am going to say it again. The blood the Lord Jesus Christ shed on the cross cleanses us from all sin and unrighteousness.[124] Every sin we have committed in the past, every sin we will commit in the future.

"Greater love has no one than this: to lay down one's life for one's friends." – John 15:13

Jesus was referencing himself and his great act of love on the cross. His atoning work on the cross for our sin, flowing out of his love for us. And while we understand the concepts of forgiveness and salvation in our mind, many of us have never forgiven ourselves and so are never free. It is not until we experience God's forgiveness through the love of Jesus Christ in our heart that we become truly free.

When you plow, you dig down into the soil of your heart. Breaking up the dry, crusty earth into smaller pieces so they may receive the light of forgiveness. It is the work of plowing that begins to let the River of Life[125] and the love of God flow into your heart. Nourishing, healing, renewing. Bringing forth life. Bringing tov!

HARROWING

"Forgiveness is the final form of love." – Reinhold Niebuhr[126]

TOV MARKER

Harrowing ensures that soil is optimally prepared for planting. Moving with God toward the creation of the tov heart, harrowing builds on the work of God's forgiveness of our sin. From the forgiveness we've received to forgiving others and asking others for forgiveness.

Having plowed the field, it must now be harrowed. Harrowing helps suppress weed growth. Creating an optimal seedbed for planting. Improving soil fertility and helping to distribute water evenly over the field. Harrowing works to increase the harvest.

As we partner with God to harrow the soil of our heart we build on the process of plowing. Taking the forgiveness we received from God and extending it to those who have sinned against us.

Before I go any farther, I want to be very, very clear—forgiveness does not equal forgetting. Forgiveness also does not ignore the sin, pain, or trauma we have experienced. Forgiveness is not unwise and is not dependent upon the repentance of the other. But it is in unforgiveness that we experience the separation from God and others that leads to emotional and spiritual death.

Emotional death keeps us bound to the world through self-centeredness and self-righteousness. Spiritual death ignores the work of Christ, the source of all true life and love, in fear and unbelief.

You will not bear the fruit God intends if you do not forgive.

We choose to forgive the sin of others against us, not to let them "off the hook" but to release our hearts from the scourge of vengeance. Vengeance ensures that another's sin continues to keep our hearts bound to the initial act of sin. Establishing a hold over our heart and a foothold for the Evil One to use against us.[127]

Jesus himself provides us an IF regarding forgiveness.

"For if you forgive others their trespasses, your heavenly Father will also forgive you, but if you do not forgive others their trespasses, neither will your Father forgive your trespasses."
– Ephesians 4:26-27

Paul also instructs us regarding forgiveness.

"Let all bitterness and wrath and anger and clamor and slander be put away from you, along with all malice. Be kind to one another, tenderhearted, forgiving one another, as God in Christ forgave you" – Ephesians 4:31-32 ESV

> *"Beloved, never avenge yourselves, but leave it to the wrath of God, for it is written, 'Vengeance is mine, I will repay,' says the Lord."*
> – Romans 12:19 ESV

On the flip side, harrowing also requires us to ask, whenever possible, for the forgiveness of those we have sinned against.

Asking for forgiveness from those we have harmed is one of the hardest things you will ever do. But it is necessary to ensure that the preparation of the soil of your hearts continues.

Jesus tells us clearly,

> *"Therefore, if you are offering your gift at the altar and there remember that your brother or sister has something against you, leave your gift there in front of the altar. First go and be reconciled to them; then come and offer your gift."*
> – Matthew 5:23-24

Forgiving others and asking others for forgiveness falls clearly within the bounds of Jesus' admonition to love others as ourselves. And Paul, in Romans 12:18, tells us that *"If it is possible, as far as it depends on you, live at peace with everyone."*

Forgiveness is not dependent upon the response of the other person. Whether giving forgiveness or asking for it, both are acts of love and obedience to God. The other's response in either case is irrelevant to the harrowing of the soil of your heart as you and God work together toward the tov heart.

LEVELING

"The path of the righteous is level; you, the Upright One, make the way of the righteous smooth." – Isaiah 26:7

TOV MARKER

Leveling creates a flat, uniform surface that increases both the yield and quality of the harvest. In the context of your story and your gifting it is redemption that levels the soil of your heart. Establishing the tov heart within you. It is this work of God within you to unite the redemption of your story and your gifting that enables the creation of environments where life flourishes. It is here, from your tov heart, that you begin to impact the world as God intends.

Leveling refers to the process of smoothing uneven or sloped land to create a flat, uniform surface. Leveling a field reduces the work required to establish and maintain a crop. Increasing both the yield and quality of the harvest while providing for improved irrigation and weed control.

Redemption is the work of God already accomplished within both your story and your gifting by the work of Christ Jesus on the cross. This is the work that brings peace, comfort, assurance, confidence, and power. That empowers you to step out into the world, in the context of God's love, to impact those around you for good.

But remember, we live in a world at war. We don't just snap our fingers and cancel the effects of the confusion, pain, trauma, loss, and abuse we have experienced. The forces set against us are real, much like drought and weeds are set against a farmer. It's a constant battle and you must fight. You must grab hold of the redemption that is objectively true. You must appropriate it and that takes time and the exercise of your will. But, if you will allow God to level the field of your heart, the outcome will be more beautiful and stranger than you could ever imagine.

In an illustrative scene from *The Chosen*,[128] the Pharisee Nicodemus has seen and experienced something he cannot explain. He is beginning to question how God works in the world, and he tries to explain it to his wife, Zohara. Taking her over to a mirror he asks,

Nicodemus: *"What do you see in the mirror?"*
Zohara: *"That is a cheap glass, I can barely make out anything at all."*
Nicodemus: *"Sometimes, I wonder if what we can know of Adonai and the Law is just as blurred. What if we're not seeing the whole picture? What if it's more beautiful and more strange than we can ever imagine?"*

The Apostle Paul echoed the same idea when he said,

"For now we see in a mirror dimly, but then face to face. Now I know in part; then I shall know fully, even as I have been fully known." – 1 Corinthians 13:12

As we work in partnership with God to level the field of our heart, we don't just seek the healing of our story and gifting. We also seek their redemption. As we step into our story and lay hold of our gifting with God, we desire, and he directs their redemption.

When Jesus started his public work of redemption, he did so by quoting from Isaiah 61. Defining the purpose of his work in the world.

> *The Spirit of the Sovereign LORD is on me,*
> *because the LORD has anointed me*
> *to proclaim good news to the poor.*
> *He has sent me to bind up the brokenhearted,*
> *to proclaim freedom for the captives*
> *and release from darkness for the prisoners,*
> *to proclaim the year of the LORD's favor*
> *and the day of vengeance of our God,*
> *to comfort all who mourn,*
> *and provide for those who grieve in Zion—*
> *to bestow on them a crown of beauty*
> *instead of ashes,*
> *the oil of joy*
> *instead of mourning,*
> *and a garment of praise*
> *instead of a spirit of despair.*
> *They will be called oaks of righteousness,*
> *a planting of the LORD*
> *for the display of his splendor.*

C.S. Lewis put it more succinctly when he said,

> *"For God is not merely mending, not simply restoring a status quo. Redeemed humanity is to be something more glorious than unfallen humanity."* – C.S. Lewis[129]

Jesus came not simply to heal humanity but to redeem it. Yes, that's it—"more glorious," more abundant...tov!

As we have previously discussed, our life is a story. For many of us, it's a story that includes pain, opposition, trauma, and fear. We desperately need healing, and as we plow and harrow with God, it is healing we will experience. But for you to be the man God created you to be and bear the fruit he intendeds, your story must be leveled. Your story must be redeemed.

The same is true of our gifting. Each of us has been uniquely gifted with talents and abilities. But for you to step into that gifting and bring forth the fruit God intended, your gifting too must be leveled. Your gifting must be redeemed.

We have already visited the redemption of our story and our gifting. But as a reminder and because it is so very important, what does it mean for our story and gifting to be redeemed?

When you can share your story with others, in truth and with integrity. Both the joy and healing along with the pain and trauma. Openly without shame or guilt. Then your story has been redeemed.

The same is true of our gifting. When you recognize, accept, and step into the gifting God created in you. Without posing or using them as a shield or club, then your gifting has been redeemed.

Please recognize that redemption too is a process and takes time. So don't rush it. Walk with God in and through this process of redemption. This process of redemption is accomplished through the movement of the Holy Spirit within your heart and mind. Allowing you to practically lay hold of what is already objectively true.

Much of this movement of the Holy Spirit in my own life has been mysterious. He has worked in the daylight and at night. Through my thoughts and my dreams, both those I remember and those I don't.

Often, I don't see or recognize the Spirit's work until one day, I notice that I am different. I don't struggle with the same things I did before.

The anger and frustration of the me-centered life is no longer there or has significantly diminished. I find my compassion for others increasing in ways I can't explain or understand. Or fear no longer controls my actions and reactions.

Don't give up just because you haven't had a "God moment." Be patient and continue to lean into him. Trust him, no matter what! He is always at work within you as he levels the field to bring the tov heart to life within you.

When our redeemed stories unite with our redeemed gifting and talent, grounded in the fullness of God's love, we become truly powerful. This is who you were created to be. This is the man God wants to release into the world. Bringing a harvest one hundred, sixty, or thirty times what was planted!

> *"'Make level paths for your feet,' so that the lame may not be disabled, but rather healed."* – Hebrews 12:13

> *"Make level paths for your feet and take only ways that are firm."*
> – Proverbs 4:26

PART FIVE

GUARDING THE TOV HEART

CHAPTER 10
REQUIRED NOURISHMENT

*"Above all else, guard your heart,
for it is the wellspring of life."*
Proverbs 4:23 NIV 1984

THE TOV HEART

CLEANING HOUSE ISN'T ENOUGH

"When an impure spirit comes out of a person, it goes through arid places seeking rest and does not find it. Then it says, 'I will return to the house I left.' When it arrives, it finds the house unoccupied, swept clean and put in order. Then it goes and takes with it seven other spirits more wicked than itself, and they go in and live there. And the final condition of that person is worse than the first. That is how it will be with this wicked generation." – Matthew 12:43-45

TOV MARKER

Cleaning up our act isn't enough. For your heart to be tov, you must let Jesus occupy it. If you don't, the Evil One and his emissaries have free reign to come back to trash the place. You must allow Jesus to inhabit every room of your heart. Forever.

This passage has been very disruptive for me. It may be one of the most disruptive passages in the New Testament.

For years, I read this passage with a big question mark hanging over it. Why, if this person cleaned up their life, were the foul spirits so easily able to return and occupy the "house"? The house, of course, being the person's heart.

Applying the measure of this verse to my own life, if I accept Jesus as my Lord and Savior, repent of my sins, and stop doing bad things, isn't that enough?

That's the "Gospel" preached in most American churches; isn't it? We are told to clean up our act, to clean house. And, yes, cleaning house is a great and necessary start, but so often we forget what the foul spirit found when it returned.

The house was empty. Unoccupied.

When a squatter looks for a house to live in, do they just barge into an occupied house and kick the owner and his family out? No, they find a house that is empty, unoccupied. Why? Because there's no resistance.

"Submit yourselves, then, to God. Resist the devil, and he will flee from you." – James 4:7

"If the Spirit of him who raised Jesus from the dead dwells in you, he who raised Christ Jesus from the dead will also give life to your mortal bodies through his Spirit who dwells in you."
– Romans 8:6-11

"To them God has chosen to make known among the Gentiles the glorious riches of this mystery, which is Christ in you, the hope of glory." – Colossians 1:27

If you are to keep the squatters from returning and destroying the house of your tov heart, it must be occupied. Jesus must dwell there for it to be safe.

This is also a great illustration of the process of truth moving from your head to your heart.

The church tells us to "clean house"—accept Jesus as Savior, repent, and stop doing bad things and then we're good to go. The implication is that everything will now be fine. And we believe it. We jump right over Jesus' warning in

Matthew 12. And then our world comes apart and we don't understand why.

There are two parts to this parable, the cleaning of the house, and the occupation.

Once we clean the house, it is crucial to let God occupy the house. Most of us don't know what that really means or, if we do glimpse the meaning, only give him a room or two. We must be intentional and persistent and learn to trust him with the whole house.

We must also be aware that there is often a hidden room behind the bookcase in the study. So, there's more work to do, deeper to go, stronger to become. More cleaning to do and more to be occupied.

The process of cleaning and occupying is lifelong. It is one of the reasons the Holy Spirit came to help us along the way. If we trust that Jesus is a good tenant and remain willing to open doors to newly discovered rooms, the Holy Spirit helps with the cleaning out so Jesus can occupy them.

Remember Paul's prayer for the Ephesians.

"Then Christ will make his home in your hearts as you trust in him..."[130]

As we are cleaning house, we must allow Christ to live in our inmost being. If we don't, it won't go well.

It is only through Christ's presence in your heart that you can *"bear much fruit"* and keep the Evil One at bay. Remember, Jesus assured us that *"apart from me you can do nothing."*[131]

The process is both grueling and beautiful. A good friend recently put it this way:

> *I've known for years that emotions can't dictate response. And in a lot of ways, I've lived that. I've kept going, kept being faithful, even when my emotions were screaming at me to stop. But in some ways, I haven't lived it. The emotions have been so strong at points that it was all I could do just to survive.*
>
> *There have been many times that I felt like I was drowning. But something about preparing and preaching Psalm 13 fortified me. I think I'm now more able to subdue them more than before, like maybe I'm stronger than my emotions for the first time in a long time.*

This is a good man, a lover of Jesus who has walked with him for many years and, in some ways, suffered much and long. Yet he continues to allow the Holy Spirit to open doors. Psalm 13 opened a door for him, but wasn't about Psalm 13 per se. It will probably be something different for you. It's not about the what, it's about the how. God directs the what, and you, like my friend, must participate in the how.

You must be willing to "get your hands dirty" to clean house. *And* you must be willing to open the door and let Jesus come in to live.

> *"Behold, I stand at the door and knock. If anyone hears my voice and opens the door, I will come in to him and eat with him, and he with me."* – Revelation 3:20 ESV

ESCAPING EXPECTATION

Shortly before dawn Jesus went out to them, walking on the lake. When the disciples saw him walking on the lake, they were terrified. "It's a ghost," they said, and cried out in fear.

But Jesus immediately said to them: "Take courage! It is I. Don't be afraid."

"Lord, if it's you," Peter replied, "tell me to come to you on the water."

"Come," he said.

Then Peter got down out of the boat, walked on the water and came toward Jesus. But when he saw the wind, he was afraid and, beginning to sink, cried out, "Lord, save me!" – Matthew 14:25–30

TOV MARKER

"Eyes on me." Jesus' three simple words of rescue that began the shift from expectation to expectancy. Expectation is based on what we know. Expectancy exists in the realm of the unknown. Expectation is practical and self-focused. Expectancy is God-focused and limitless. The shift changes the way you view yourself and others, what you believe is possible. Far above and beyond the limitations of what we expect.

Remember the three words Jesus gave me as a mighty, permanent rescue. They have taken root in my heart as an intricate part of the abundant life he is building in me.

Eyes on me.

These three simple words fundamentally changed my perspective and posture as I navigated the trauma, loss, and pain of COVID life. The relational, social, and spiritual fallout associated with it. These three words, while a rescue in and of themselves, have also been the foundation for the migration of my heart's posture from expectation to expectancy.

We have a lot of expectations. Based on our circumstances, our expectations may seem good (job advancement, solid relationships, a nice little life) or not so good (crappy job, no friends, stuck where I am, financial or health challenges). However, there is one thing all expectations have in common. They are born of self. They are all about us.

Even the expectations we hold for others are all about what we expect. Our expectations are all about what we hope for or what we fear based upon what we believe we or others are capable of.

For the majority of my life, I have lived with expectations, and most of those have been good. My circumstances have been such that I have experienced career growth, generally good relationships and health, and, for the most part, a happy little life. A life grounded in what I could see as possible based on my hard work and the gifts and capabilities God gave me.

Now, I am not saying that my life has been all roses and lollipops. I have had my share of failure, disappointment, and pain. Fatherlessness (parents divorced when I was three), two years of unemployment, and failed relationships testify to that. But for the most part, things have gone okay. But is "okay" what Jesus promised?

> "I came that they may have life and have it abundantly."
> – John 10:10 ESV

Jesus didn't promise us a happy little life, he promised abundance. And not abundance only in the life to come but also in the here and now.

If we are honest with ourselves, the abundant life Jesus promises in this world is an enigma. The idea of living an abundant life in this world is confusing and mysterious. Frustrating and enticing.

Abundant life is also opposed by, among other things, our expectations. Our expectations are all "down to earth," for ourselves and others, based on what we see as possible. Our understanding of our circumstances, abilities, history, and opportunities. Or how we view the circumstances, abilities, history, and opportunities of others.

In Ephesians 3, Paul seeks to move us beyond expectation into a way of living that makes abundant life possible. From expectation to expectancy.

> "Now to him who is able to do immeasurably more than all we ask or imagine, according to his power that is at work within us, to him be glory in the church and in Christ Jesus throughout all generations, for ever and ever! Amen." – Ephesians 3:20-21

I find it interesting that when Paul arrives here in prayer, he has just finished surfing the immense sea of language in an attempt to describe the vastness of the love of God. And then, in the shadow of God's love, he leads us into the realm of expectancy.

Yes, expectation and expectancy are similar, but their focus is very different. Expectation is based upon what I believe is possible in the context of living my life. Expectancy is rooted in faith and what I can't see. Expectancy is present in the unknown. In the assurance of what is not currently seen or experienced. As the writer of Hebrews said,

> "*Now faith is being sure of what we hope for and certain of what we do not see.*" – Hebrews 11:1 NIV 1984

As Jesus makes his home in our heart and tov becomes a way of life, our perspective transitions from expectation to expectancy. Our perspective shifts. Our days start not with "*How can I make this or that happen (or prevent it from happening)?*" but with "*Jesus, where are we going today? What are you going to do? And how do you want me to participate?*"

As we embrace the move from expectation to expectancy the posture of our heart shifts. From looking at the world in terms of what we know is possible, to trusting God to show up in beautiful, powerful, unknown, and unexpected ways. When the posture of our heart moves from expectation to expectancy, tov becomes real. We begin to look forward to what God, in his infinite love and with his unlimited resources, is going to do in and through us and others each day.

"*Eyes on me.*" Three little words of rescue. Three little words of guidance. Three little words that shifted how I see myself and the way I perceive others. It may seem like a subtle shift, but at the core of my being, the shift has been life changing. A shift that leads to freedom and restores life. A shift that strengthens relationships. A shift toward faith and trust, grounded in love and hope. A shift that stirs within me the promise of outcomes far above and beyond the limits of my expectations.

> *"So we fix our eyes not on what is seen, but on what is unseen, since what is seen is temporary, but what is unseen is eternal."*
> – 2 Corinthians 4:18

> *"I pray that the eyes of your heart may be enlightened in order that you may know the hope to which he has called you, the riches of his glorious inheritance in his holy people..."*
> – Ephesians 1:18

A WORD ON SUFFERING

"The absence of tumult, more than its presence, is an enemy of the soul. God meets you in your weakness, not in your strength. He comforts those who mourn, not those who live above desperation. He reveals Himself more often in darkness than in the happy moments of life."
– Dan B. Allender[132]

TOV MARKER

Suffering is a given in this world and can take many forms. How we respond to suffering is different from anyone else. We must honor another person's experience of it as we honor our own. Suffering also leads to either despair or hope. In suffering we must make a choice, turn our backs on God or lean into him. Even when you can't see or don't understand you must guard your heart and trust Jesus. No matter what.

There are many kinds of suffering in the world. There is suffering that breaks your heart, the Shabar in Scripture, literally to pieces. There is suffering that gnaws at you day in and day out, so we grin and bear it, stuff it down, and ignore it. Crying out to God, "WHY!" And in this fallen world, there is everything between.

Suffering can be short-term or long-term. Short-term suffering hurts. The death of a family member or friend, the loss of a job, or change in the economy that makes it impossible to make ends meet. Long-term suffering brings our deepest questions to the surface. The "*why?*" questions. A chronic illness or debilitating accident, addictions both personal and in those around us, or jobs we hate but are chained to because, well, others depend on us.

Yet the interesting thing about suffering is that how you respond to it is as unique as your story. There are things I experience that devastate me, but if they were to happen to you, you might not blink. The reverse is also true; things that shake you to the core I might handle with an honest air of "*I am okay.*"

Dan Allender puts it this way, "*Don't diminish anyone else's pain.*" We must honor ourselves and others, especially when it comes to pain and suffering.

When we suffer, it is hard to see the end of the rainbow or the light at the end of the tunnel. Too often it is a dark place, a place of fear and dread and, sometimes, despair.

It is the place of Ecclesiastes. It is the place where we must make a choice—resignation or hope. Moving toward resignation leads to suicide. Moving toward hope leads ultimately to tov and abundant life.

Even in our suffering, we have a choice. Suffering can push us to despair. But "to despair is to turn your back on God."[133]

To turn away from God amid your suffering is to remove yourself from your only true source of hope.

It is also important, and this is especially true in the middle of suffering, not to let anyone else's experience of God diminish your own. We tend to measure ourselves against the blessing we see others experiencing.

Measurement and comparison are forms of separation the Evil One uses to put distance between us and others.

Between us and God. We'll discuss that more in the next chapter. For now, guard your heart, love Jesus, and trust him. Even in your suffering. Even when you can't see the end. No matter what.

> *"Recovering from suffering is not like recovering from a disease. Many people don't come out healed; they come out different."*
> – David Brooks[134]

> *"I have told you these things, so that in me you may have peace. In this world you will have trouble. But take heart! I have overcome the world."* – John 16:33

CHAPTER 11

UNDERSTANDING THE OPPOSITION

*"Open war is upon you;
whether you'd risk it or not."*

ARAGORN,
THE LORD OF THE RINGS: THE TWO TOWERS

FIGHTING THE WRONG BATTLE

"Don't forget who the real enemy is!" – various characters to Katniss, *The Hunger Games: Catching Fire*[135]

TOV MARKER

Spiritual warfare is real and, according to scripture, a normal part of the Christian life. As in human wars, it is easy, in the heat of battle, to get confused, separated, and disoriented. If you are not careful, you can lose connection with your commander - Jesus. It is also easy to forget which battle you're fighting. The only battle you face is the one immediately before you. You will be tempted to shift your focus away from the real enemy. But remember, Eyes on Jesus ... no matter what!

"The fog of war." The term primarily applies to the experience of individual soldiers in battle. Pure confusion about direction, location, and perspective on a battlefield. Officers and soldiers become separated. Orders become confused and subject to revision due to poor communication. Sounds and vision are limited and may not be easily resolved. The result being continuing uncertainty, a perceptual "fog."[136]

In the fog of war, between the traumatic abuse of sight and sound, the body pumping adrenaline, and the nearness of death, it's easy to forget who the real enemy is.

The same is true with spiritual warfare.

The urgency of our need and the multifaceted nature of the attack create confusion. Goals and objectives get blurred. Communication with God gets muffled and disrupted. Fear, confusion, misunderstanding, and frustration lead us into a posture of inaction.

Under these circumstances, it is easy to mistake friend for foe and enemy for ally. If we are to live out of the tov heart and step into the abundant life Jesus promised, we must understand the nature of our opposition and how to recognize what is coming against us.

Fortunately, the Apostle Paul provides two additional clear guides to keep us from dashing ourselves upon the rocks of this fallen world in the midst of the battle. Ways to recognize our enemies in the heat of battle and through the fog of war.

> *"...the fruit of the Spirit is love, joy, peace, patience, kindness, goodness, faithfulness, gentleness and self-control..."*
> – Ephesians 5:22–23

> *"...there is now no condemnation for those who are in Christ Jesus, because through Christ Jesus the law of the Spirit who gives life has set you free from the law of sin and death."*
> – Romans 8:1–2

No matter what is going on in your life, if you gauge the outcome against these guides, you can successfully navigate the assault.

If what is presenting itself to you brings love, joy, peace, patience, kindness, goodness, faithfulness, gentleness, and

THE TOV HEART

self-control, lean into it, even if it is hard or challenging. It is from God.

If you experience condemnation, fear, anger, diminishment, or confusion, go to war against it.

You have three forces of darkness set against the tov heart and abundant life—The World, The Flesh, and The Devil.

They are set against the person God created you to be, the man he wishes to use to impact the world. The more we move to align ourselves with the tov heart God is creating within us, the more the attack intensifies. Remember, every movement toward God will be opposed.

These dark forces are each a unique foe, bent either on their own supremacy or our destruction with the ultimate goal of separation. Separation from God and separation from others.

As you step into the battle, it is crucial to remember that you are not who you used to be and that your battle is before you, not behind you.

> *"...if anyone is in Christ, he is a new creation; the old has gone, the new has come!"* – 2 Corinthians 5:17 NIV 1984

In 2016, director Antoine Fuqua remade the 1960 western *The Magnificent Seven*.[137] As the seven unlikely allies are preparing for the battle to save the town of Rose Creek from an evil robber baron, one of the seven allies, Goodnight Robicheaux, is concerned that their leader, Sam Chisolm, is living out of his traumatic past. Goodnight knows that for them to have any chance to succeed against such long odds, Chisholm must be present to the battle before them, and so he asks him why they are in this fight. When Chisholm pushes back on the question, Goodnight responds,

> *"Just making sure we're fighting the battle in front of us, not behind."*

Regardless of who you were, you must remain present to who Jesus has created you to be. Who you've become and who you are becoming. What you were is important to your story but only without the shame and guilt, the diminishment and oppression that accompanies the "old man." Your past has been redeemed, and who you are and who you're becoming is who Jesus wants to use to impact the world.

Letting go of who you were is a choice, a choice for freedom over bondage, life over death. It's hard to let go of the pain, fear, and trauma of what we've done and what has been done to us. But you must let it go if you are to be the man Jesus created you to be. The reality is that we can only fight the battles in front of us. It is the only place we can live, each moment of each day. The choices, decisions, and actions that matter are *now*.

It is not who you were but who you are and who you are becoming. And the battle is in front of you, not behind. Eyes on Jesus. Trusting. No matter what.

THE WORLD

> *"You adulterous people, don't you know that friendship with the world means enmity against God? Therefore, anyone who chooses to be a friend of the world becomes an enemy of God."* – James 4:4

TOV MARKER

The World is anything in the culture that entices you to put your hope in or reliance on anything other than God. Today, the gateway to The World is the Internet. The Internet as arbiter of knowledge and truth. Scripture on the other hand tells us to "trust in the Lord with all our heart" for if we don't, well, "Remember Lot's wife."

When James speaks here of the "world," he does not mean God's creation—oceans, mountains, plains, animals, plant life, fishes, and certainly not humanity. John 3:16 is a high and true beacon of the love of God for his creation and, most importantly, for humanity:

> *"For God so loved the world that he gave his one and only Son, that whoever believes in him shall not perish but have eternal life."*

Remember, God pronounced all his creation to be tov. Fully capable of performing its purpose and design in creation. Recreating itself, as God intended, to create exponentially more life.

UNDERSTANDING THE OPPOSITION

The world James is speaking of here and that I am referencing is the antithesis of life.

The World as I use it here and as has been expressed by many saints throughout the ages[138] may be quite simply summarized as,

> *Anything in the culture that entices you to put your hope in or reliance on anything other than God.*

The ways and enticements of The World are many and varied. But, the primary manifestation of The World is through the Internet. Not the technology, the content.

For the most part, the sum of all human knowledge is today, true and untrue, found on *"The Internet."* Through the Internet, the forces of darkness prey on the insatiable human desire for answers driven by our broken need to control and manage our lives. Our pain and trauma, the outcomes of our interactions with others, and the primary human drug of choice—our happiness.

> *"All men seek happiness. This is without exception. Whatever different means they employ, they all tend to this end. The cause of some going to war, and of others avoiding it, is the same desire in both, attended with different views. The will never takes the least step but to this object. This is the motive of every action of every man, even of those who hang themselves."*
> – Blaise Pascal[139]

So, we search for knowledge, answers to the questions of our lives. And because we are busy, tired, impatient, and lazy, we go to the most readily available source. Take the path of least resistance, the Internet. After all, we, very literally, hold the sum of all human knowledge in the palm of our hand. Pause and let that sink in for a minute.

Let me ask you a question, *When was the last time you opened a book to get an answer?* To get clarity or understanding? How about counsel or advice? Is your *"go–to"* your circle of friends and a conversation? A manual or written instructions? Or, is it the Internet?

Don't get me wrong here. I use the Internet. I am not saying don't use it. The Internet is a tool and can be a very useful one. Answers are good, generally speaking. We need answers and getting them quickly and efficiently is helpful. But when we have trained ourselves to believe that the Internet is the arbiter of knowledge and truth in our lives, it becomes a problem.

The exclusivity of the Internet regarding the acquisition of the content we use to govern our lives, no matter what the source, is dangerous and can be deceptive.

The Word of God tells us clearly,

"Trust in the Lord with all your heart and lean not on your own understanding; in all your ways acknowledge him, and he will make your paths straight." – Proverbs 3:5-6 NIV 1984

Jesus himself told us,

"I am the way and the truth and the life" – John 14:6a

In Luke 17, Jesus speaks directly about the temptation of The World and the resulting consequences of choosing The World over himself.

> *Just as it was in the days of Noah, so also will it be in the days of the Son of Man. People were eating, drinking, marrying and being given in marriage up to the day Noah entered the ark. Then the flood came and destroyed them all.*
>
> *It was the same in the days of Lot. People were eating and drinking, buying and selling, planting and building. But the day Lot left Sodom, fire and sulfur rained down from heaven and destroyed them all.*
>
> *It will be just like this on the day the Son of Man is revealed. On that day no one who is on the housetop, with possessions inside, should go down to get them. Likewise, no one in the field should go back for anything. Remember Lot's wife! Whoever tries to keep their life will lose it, and whoever loses their life will preserve it.* – John 17:26-33

Jesus tells us, in normal, everyday life, to "remember Lot's wife." But why? If you recall the story from Genesis 19, God had determined to destroy Sodom and Gomorrah. However, loving Lot and his family, God sent two angels to Sodom to warn them to flee and lead them out of the city. As soon as they were outside the city, one of the angels implored them to run for their lives and warning them not to look back.[140]

But as burning sulfur rained down on the city behind her, Lot's wife looked back and became a pillar of salt. She looked back. She chose what she was told to leave behind. She chose her past life. She chose The World. She chose the battle behind her. She chose Sodom...and lost it all.

> "*Do not love the world or anything in the world. If anyone loves the world, love for the Father is not in them.*" – 1 John 2:15

> "*Whoever tries to keep their life will lose it, and whoever loses their life will preserve it.*" – Luke 17:32–33

THE FLESH

"*For the wages of sin is death...*" – Romans 6:23a

TOV MARKER

The Flesh is the pull of our sin nature that takes us into self. Self-reliance, self-gratification, and self-medication. When we take the deep questions of our lives to anyone or anything other than God for comfort or solace, we enter the "Hotel California"[141] of sin. It is only through the atoning work of the Lord Jesus Christ on the cross and our willingness to accept that work that your heart becomes tov.

Unfortunately, we are all too familiar with The Flesh. We've lived with it all our lives. The sin nature, born of Adam and Eve's rebellion in the Garden of Eden. The Flesh is primarily, but not exclusively, what the work of Jesus Christ on the cross addressed.

> "When you were dead in your sins and in the uncircumcision of your flesh, God made you alive with Christ. He forgave us all our sins, having canceled the charge of our legal indebtedness, which stood against us and condemned us; he has taken it away, nailing it to the cross." – Colossians 2:13-14

Simply defined, The Flesh is the pull of our sin nature that takes us to self-reliance, self-gratification, or self-medication.

We rely on many things in this life—our work, the money we make, our wife or girlfriend, or even the pain we feel.

For most of my life, even as a Christian, I relied on two things. My ability to figure things out and get things done, and the validation I received from romantic relationships.

The first was born of my orphan heart and the decreation of my God-given gifting. The second was born of my desperate need for validation as a man. The result was extreme self-reliance and taking my question about my value as a man to the woman.

God gifted me with the ability to figure things out in the world. Whether at work or at home, technical or physical, rational or spiritual, I could figure it out. This gifting was meant to be used in a close walk with Jesus to draw me into union with him. To help others do the same. To create an environment where life could flourish.

Instead, in my flesh, I warped my gifting into a dependence on myself apart from Jesus and I became a loner. A very capable man who was able to make his life work without God even as I professed him as Lord and Savior.

We men all have the same basic question, *"Do I have what it takes?"* That question can only be truly answered in union with God through Jesus. But like most men, I went elsewhere for my answer. Some take their question to their work. Some take it to sports. Some to pornography, drugs, or alcohol. I took it to the woman. As a result, if the relationship I was in was going well, I was well. If it was not going well, I was not. I place my identity as a man on the quicksand of another human being's brokenness.

I learned to hide the impact from others around me, but the emotional swings in my heart when I was alone were, to say the least, painful and confusing.

It may be different for you. It probably is. But your experience of the flesh can be found first and foremost in where you put your trust and where you've grounded your identity.

Too often, we turn to other comforters. Some are subtle. Video games, Instagram, Facebook, and TikTok. Binging sports or the latest TV series. Or, long hours at work. Some comforters are not so subtle. Alcohol, drugs, or sex.

We choose distraction and relief. Comfort over restoration and renewal.

My client Sanju's struggle is what he does with his loneliness and stress. For him, distraction and relief have been found in porn. It has become, as with most distraction and relief, an addiction. Tied to his sexual identity, the tentacles of the addiction have dug deep into his being. His flesh warps his perception of his identity, leading to deep-seated guilt and shame which The Devil has used to keep him bound, confused, and frustrated.

We also really like Psalm 37:4,

"Take delight in the Lord, and he will give you the desires of your heart."

As Christians, we love to lean into the last part of that verse. Being given the desires of our heart sounds like a dream come true! But we ignore the command, *"Take delight in the Lord."* Not just acknowledge him or read your Bible everyday but *delight*!

Or, depending on our church background, we lean hard into Jeremiah 17:9.

"The heart is deceitful above all things and beyond cure. Who can understand it?"

The truth is yes and no. Yes, the Lord will give you the desires of your heart. Your true heart. Your tov heart, full of the Spriit of God.

"I will give you a new heart and put a new spirit in you; I will remove from you your heart of stone and give you a heart of flesh. And I will put my Spirit in you and move you to follow my decrees and be careful to keep my laws."
– Ezekiel 36:26-27

Ezekiel prophesied the surgical work of God in us, through Christ Jesus, to give us a new heart. Not our old heart refurbished like a used computer or car, but a completely new heart. A heart transplant. A heart aligned with the Spirit of God. And in the Spirit of God, the desires of our heart take on new meaning and fresh substance. Not in rejecting who you are, but in the redemption and recreation of who he intended when he created you.

The rejection of self and The Flesh requires us to recognize our need. And, in doing so, we echo David's prayer in Psalm 51:10-12:

> "*Create in me a pure heart, O God, and renew a steadfast spirit within me. Do not cast me from your presence or take your Holy Spirit from me. Restore to me the joy of your salvation and grant me a willing spirit, to sustain me.*"

The rejection of self and The Flesh can only be accomplished through our willingness and Christ's atoning, redemptive work on the cross. It is only in the context of the tov heart that our desires can be worthy of God's provision of abundant life.

THE DEVIL

"Now the serpent was more crafty than any of the wild animals the Lord God had made. He said to the woman, 'Did God really say, "You must not eat from any tree in the garden"?'" – Genesis 3:1

TOV MARKER

The Devil is the active being opposed to God. An opportunist, his single goal is separation. To separate you from God and from others through lies and deception. Luckily the Apostles provide ways to resist him and his emissaries and stand firm in your faith. You will also be more able to withstand what The Devil throws against you if you have brothers in Christ Jesus who will fight by your side and on your behalf. Search them out, nurture these relationships. You can never have too many allies!

The Devil, also called Satan, Lucifer and the Evil One, depicted as a serpent or snake in the Bible—accuser or adversary in Hebrew—is the active being opposed to God. Cast out of heaven actively and maliciously acting to separate us from God and from each other.

The Devil is an opportunist, and he acts with malice toward God and his people with a single goal in mind. Separation. His sole purpose, regardless of the specific method or form of attack, is, at its core, to separate us from God and from each other.

In the Garden, The Devil asked Eve a simple question, and in doing so, sowed doubt as a way to separate her from God.

The tactic is simple and cunning. The attacks of The Devil and his emissaries—generally termed demons or foul or unclean spirits[142]—take advantage of both the pull of the world and brokenness of the flesh.

The interactions are dynamic and complex, but it is important to realize one thing. No matter what happens or what the actual cause is, The Devil and his emissaries will always put their spin on it. The spin will be toward deception and will initially have enough truth woven in to make it sound plausible. And, if possible, will attempt to cast doubt on the trustworthiness of God.

A good friend of mine, Robert, has been hurt badly by people in the church. People he had grown to love and trust, people he had opened up to and shared much of his "*dirty*" past with.

But the tide turned, and he was disrespected, diminished, and, yes, even abused. The dynamics and particulars don't really matter here other than to say that the work of The Flesh in others overflowed into malice, hatred, and gossip against Robert, creating separation to the point where he is afraid to go to church.

For many in Robert's situation—especially since he is a relatively new Christian—there would also be separation from God. But to Robert's credit and by God's grace, he has remained a strong follower of Jesus, despite the attack.

However, the ramifications have not just affected Robert. As so often happens, they have spread. The situation has been noticed by members of Robert's family, and, as a result, the family has also separated from the church.

For Robert, the betrayal by these close friends in the church led to diminishment, shame, guilt, and a questioning of purpose fueled by his own brokenness and flesh. A toxic confusion of attack against his gifting led to isolation. The good news is that he is working through recovery and forgiveness with Jesus and some others who have come alongside him.

I relate this story for a couple of reasons. First, I believe many of us have had a similar experience at some point in our walk with Jesus in the church. Second, I am sure that The Devil and his emissaries, while not directly causing this, put their spin on the situation and fanned the flames of the brokenness of the flesh in an attempt to separate this man from God and from others.

This is why we are given strong warnings by three of the Apostles:

"Submit yourselves, then, to God. Resist the devil, and he will flee from you." – James 4:7

"Put on the full armor of God, so that you can take your stand against the devil's schemes. For our struggle is not against flesh and blood, but against the rulers, against the authorities, against the powers of this dark world and against the spiritual forces of evil in the heavenly realms. Therefore put on the full armor of God, so that when the day of evil comes, you may be able to stand your ground, and after you have done everything, to stand." – Ephesians 6:11-13

"Be alert and of sober mind. Your enemy the devil prowls around like a roaring lion looking for someone to devour. Resist

> *him, standing firm in the faith, because you know that the family of believers throughout the world is undergoing the same kind of sufferings. And the God of all grace, who called you to his eternal glory in Christ, after you have suffered a little while, will himself restore you and make you strong, firm and steadfast."*
> – 1 Peter 5:8–10

James is matter of fact and to the point, submit to God and resist the devil. No submit. No resist. No flee.

Paul addresses both the earthly and heavenly dimensions of the battle we face with The Devil and his emissaries, along with how to proactively defend ourselves.

Lastly, Peter. You can tell he's been there, done that. This is a man who has experienced the attack of The Devil in concert with The Flesh and The World. This is also a man who has repented, returned his eyes to Jesus, and been restored. He knows these attacks are common to every believer, and he also knows we need encouragement.

So often, it seems like we're alone, without allies, left to figure it out ourselves. That too is a lie of The Devil, to keep us from looking for allies, in whom we find strength and encouragement.

> *"... standing firm in the faith, because you know that the family of believers throughout the world is undergoing the same kind of sufferings."*

The lie also keeps us acknowledging the truth of Christ's work and his presence in us.

"And the God of all grace, who called you to his eternal glory in Christ, after you have suffered a little while, will himself restore you and make you strong, firm and steadfast."

When you are attacked, you're not blowing it, and you are not alone. Resist and stand firm! Search high and low for allies. For yourself and for others in Christ Jesus!

CHAPTER 12
BELAYED & BELAYING

Belaying is the process used to keep a climber from falling too far by applying friction on the rope. The system includes rope, anchors, a belay device, and a belayer. A belayer is the person who manages the rope to catch the climber on the other end in case of a fall or a slip.

ROPE

> *"'Rope!' muttered Sam. 'I knew I'd want it, if I hadn't got it!'"*
> – Sam Gamgee, *The Fellowship of the Ring*, J.R.R. Tolkien

TOV MARKER

It is a climber's trust in his rope that provides the confidence they need to scale the heights or plumb the depths of the earth. In the same way, God's Hope, Love, and Word are woven together into a rope of life that will never fail and in which we can trust. No matter what.

When I was a teenager, one of my first jobs was for an organization called BoatUS. They provided a wide range of benefits, services, and products to the boating public. One product was specialty rope—anchor and docking lines. As it turned out, I was one of the people who made them at their headquarters in Alexandria, VA. Made of polyester or nylon, there were always three strands. Twisted together. A biblical precedent, whether conscious or not.

> *"Though one may be overpowered, two can defend themselves. A cord of three strands is not quickly broken."*
> – Ecclesiastes 4:12

I don't know if the ropemakers had King Solomon's words in mind, but the practicality has been clear for centuries.

Three strands twisted together, entwined, is much stronger than three alone. The twisting makes the rope stronger by ensuring the tension is evenly distributed among the individual strands.

As I made docking and anchor lines, I braided the three strands together, sealed, and wrapped them. This ensured they were even stronger; secured and sealed to survive the rigors of marine use.

Our members trusted both our rope and the specialty lines I created to be reliable and dependable. Whether in calm or stormy seas, our rope could be trusted to be there for them.

In the same way, God's Hope, Love, and Word are entwined to provide us with the ultimate rope of trust.

The Hebrew word *Tikvah*, usually translated as hope, means "chord" or "rope" and comes from its root word meaning "to bind."

> "'For I know the plans I have for you,' declares the Lord, 'plans for welfare and not for evil, to give you a future and a hope [Tikvah].'"
> – Jeremiah 29:11

God's love is steadfast and secure, something upon which we can depend no matter what comes.

> "The steadfast love of the Lord never ceases; his mercies never come to an end; they are new every morning; great is your faithfulness."
> – Lamentations 3:21-23 ESV

God's Word is living and powerful, true and eternal.

> *"For the word of God is alive and active. Sharper than any double-edged sword, it penetrates even to dividing soul and spirit, joints and marrow; it judges the thoughts and attitudes of the heart."*
> – Hebrews 4:12

> *"... so is my word that goes out from my mouth: It will not return to me empty, but will accomplish what I desire and achieve the purpose for which I sent it."* – Isaiah 55:11

> *"'Is not my word like fire,' declares the Lord, 'and like a hammer that breaks a rock in pieces?'"* – Jeremiah 23:29

> *"All your words are true; all your righteous laws are eternal."*
> – Psalm 119:160

> *"Heaven and earth will pass away, but my words will never pass away."* – Matthew 24:35

God's rope of trust, composed of Hope, Love, and the Word, is your ultimate source of security and strength. Reliable in every circumstance.

For any climber, it is trust in their rope that provides them with the confidence to scale the heights or plumb the depths of the earth. Trust in God—Father, Jesus, Holy Spirit—is your rope, strong and secure, powerful and reliable, true and eternal.

The rope of God's Hope, Love, and Word will never fail. No matter what!

ANCHORS

"The intention of an anchor is case-specific but is usually for fall protection, primarily fall arrest and fall restraint."[143]

TOV MARKER

Anchors provide a climber with protection against plummeting to the ground. God provides two strong anchors – his Promises and his Oath – to catch us when we lose our footing or grip and begin to plummet. Dependable and sure protection from death in the folly of our lives.

In climbing, anchors are a crucial component of the climbing system, providing protection for the climber in the event of a fall. The instruction for implementing anchor protection for climbing is voluminous. But, suffice it to say that anchors are of critical importance to the safety of the climber. Arresting their fall and keeping them from falling to their death.

Anchors are no less important as we live out the abundant life through our tov heart.

The writer of Hebrews provides a pair of anchors that together provide what he calls an "anchor" for the soul.

> *When God made his promise to Abraham, since there was no one greater for him to swear by, he swore by himself, saying, "I will surely bless you and give you many descendants." And so, after waiting patiently, Abraham received what was promised.*

> *People swear by someone greater than themselves, and the oath confirms what is said and puts an end to all argument. Because God wanted to make the unchanging nature of his purpose very clear to the heirs of what was promised, he confirmed it with an oath. God did this so that, by two unchangeable things in which it is impossible for God to lie, we who have fled to take hold of the hope set before us may be greatly encouraged. We have this hope as an anchor for the soul, firm and secure. It enters the inner sanctuary behind the curtain, where our forerunner, Jesus, has entered on our behalf.* – Hebrews 6:13–20

There are two anchors here, working together to provide us with safety when we fall; and fall we will.

Falling is a given in the Christian life, even as we live out abundant life through the tov heart. Adam's sin and the resulting brokenness and opposition previously discussed ensure that falling is inevitable. Even the Apostle Paul, speaking of his own sin as he lived out abundant life, said:

> *"I do not understand what I do. For what I want to do I do not do, but what I hate I do."* – Romans 7:15

Many of the heroes of the Bible fell. Adam and Eve walked with God himself in the cool of the garden, and they fell. David fell ... a lot—adultery, murder, betrayal. Elijah fell immediately after experiencing the majestic power of God that killed four hundred priests of Baal. James and John, the "Sons of Thunder," fell in their anger and pride. Peter fell when he denied Jesus. Not once, but three times. Paul himself, as he himself confessed, had a recurring failure.

Every saint down through the ages falls at some point. We're not perfect, but it is our calling to do all we can to be so. As Francis Schaeffer put it:

> *"It is our calling until He comes back again that happy day, to do all we can—while it won't be perfect as when He comes back—to see substantial healing in every area that He will then perfectly heal."*[144]

Substantial healing in every area of our lives. Not perfect, substantial. I don't know about you, but I want as much "substantial" as I can get!

I want to be the man God created me to be, the man Jesus died, was resurrected, and ascended for. When I fall, the descent stops. Arrested by two powerful anchors working together to ensure I stay firmly grounded in Jesus, God's Promises and God's Oath.

God's Promises are a steady, mighty river flowing throughout Scripture. From the Abrahamic Covenant in Genesis 12:2-3 to God's promise to Israel in Leviticus 26:12-13. From God's promise of protection and guidance in the Psalms[145] and Proverbs to his unfailing love[146] and restoration.[147] God's promises flow through the prophets (Isaiah, Jeremiah, Ezekiel, Malachi, etc.) and into the Gospels, on through the Apostles, abundantly overflowing in Jesus' final words in Scripture as our ultimate hope: "Yes, I am coming soon."[148]

An oath is a promise with maximum emphasis, a promise made in front of the most powerful person around. In God's case, his promises are oaths set before his people in front of himself. It is in and through God himself that these promises are unchangeable, immovable, and steadfast—forever!

God's Promises, made with his Oath, in and through his Word and the person of the Lord Jesus Christ, provide secure anchors of our souls. Keeping us from a complete loss of heart when we fall. They are reliable and dependable assurance. Arresting your fall. Protecting you from death in your folly.

BELAY DEVICES

> "Belay devices act as a friction brake, so that when a climber falls with any slack in the rope, the fall is brought to a stop."[149]

TOV MARKER

It is belay devices that slow and arrest a climber's descent when they fall. In the same way, God provides belay devices for your tov heart, through the Holy Spirit, as we ascend to live life abundantly.

While anchors keep a climber from falling all the way to the ground. A climber who loses their footing can freefall quite a distance before the slack in their rope is stopped by an anchor. A lot of damage can occur on the way down. Impact with ledges and outcrops, not to mention the abrupt, bone jarring stop when the climber gets to the "end of their rope." If the climber is lucky, it's just scrapes and bruises. In the worst cases, it can be broken bones, gashes, and internal injuries. All are painful and need substantial recovery time. Some may be life threatening.

To prevent severe damage, slow gravity-assisted decent, and minimize the time to recover, belay devices are used to put friction on the rope. Gripping it to restrict and slow the climber's fall thus minimizing damage.

The same is true in our ascent to the abundant life. When we fall—and we will fall—it is a freefall of the heart. The damage to our tov heart, our relationship with God, and our experience of abundant life can be no less severe.

There are many types of belay devices used in climbing. But I want to focus on one very important set of belay devices the Holy Spirit creates for your tov heart. These belay devices provide the resistance necessary to restrict our freefall of the heart.

These are my primary go-to when The World and the assault get crazy during my climb, and I sense I am losing my grip. The Fruit of the Spirit.

The *Fruit of the Spirit* are the characteristics that secure your tov heart to your trust in Christ Jesus. Connecting God's provision with your inner restoration resulting in overflow into the world around us. It is the work of the Holy Spirit in us that grounds our tov hearts in the experience of abundant life.

> "*But the fruit of the Spirit is love, joy, peace, patience, kindness, goodness, faithfulness, gentleness and self-control. Against such things there is no law.*" – Galatians 5:22-23

All of the teaching I have received about the Fruit of the Spirit has treated each fruit as a singular, isolated benefit of the Spirit of God. The Holy Spirit, dwelling in us. Good stuff and something we can all rejoice in receiving.

But what if they are not singular and isolated? What if the *Fruit of the Spirit* are interconnected, additive, and marvelously interwoven by God to firmly establish us in abundant life?

When the Holy Spirit indwells you, a process begins. It is not random or piecemeal but very deliberate and controlled. If you cooperate, it produces in you a "new creation" as part of your tov heart to make a way into abundance.

> *"Therefore, if anyone is in Christ, he is a new creation. The old has passed away; behold, the new has come."*
> – 2 Corinthians 5:17 ESV

There are nine fruit that the Holy Spirit creates in us as a way to abundant life. The first three provide a foundation for our relationship with God. The second three provide a foundation for our relationship with others. And the last three overflow through us, into the world, as we create environments where life flourishes.

Love

The Beatles sang, *"All you need is love."* Well, that's not entirely true. But love is the unmovable foundation that connects your tov heart to the tov heart of God and nourishes and sustains abundant life.

> *"So we have come to know and to believe the love that God has for us. God is love, and whoever abides in love abides in God, and God abides in him. By this is love perfected with us, so that we may have confidence for the day of judgment, because as he is so also are we in this world."* – 1 John 4:16–17 ESV

Love is the first deposit the Holy Spirit makes in us upon receiving Jesus as Lord and Savior. It is the personal, intimate knowledge that God loves you above all things and loved you first. That seed then germinates and becomes our love of God. This, in turn, overflows to become deep love for others.

> *Jesus answered, "The most important is, Hear, O Israel: The Lord our God, the Lord is one. And you shall love the Lord your God with all your heart and with all your soul and with all your mind and with all your strength. The second is this: You shall love your neighbor as yourself. There is no other commandment greater than these."* – Mark 12:29–31 ESV

Joy

Out of our love for God and others, the Spirit deposits joy.

> *"Then he said to them, 'Go your way. Eat the fat and drink sweet wine and send portions to anyone who has nothing ready, for this day is holy to our Lord. And do not be grieved, for the joy of the Lord is your strength.'"* – Nehemiah 8:10

On the foundation of love, the Spirit lays joy. Not joy as some perceive it, equal to happiness. But joy as in the solid assurance of the goodness and provision of God. The "*Blessed Assurance*" the blind hymn writer Fanny Crosby wrote about. Joy as the unshakable confidence in the one who will never leave you or forsake you.[150] Assurance and confidence fashioned by and secured in pure, steadfast, absolute love.

Peace

Following love and joy, the Spirit deposits peace.

> *"And the peace of God, which surpasses all understanding, will guard your hearts and your minds in Christ Jesus."*
> – Philippians 4:7

> *"I have said these things to you, that in me you may have peace. In the world you will have tribulation. But take heart; I have overcome the world."* – John 16:33

The union of love and joy necessarily creates peace. If God is for us, who can be against us?[151] In the presence of God's great love for us, the knowledge that we are wanted and redeemed at a cost beyond imagining, and in the resulting joy, the acceptance of and abiding in that love, the Spirit deposits peace. This is our ability to remain calm and present when all around us is in chaos.

> *"May the God of hope fill you with all joy and peace as you trust in him, so that you may overflow with hope by the power of the Holy Spirit."* – Romans 15:13

Love, Joy, and Peace—interconnected, additive, and interwoven. The wellspring of your union with God and essential to abundant life.

Pause

I want you to pause here. Take a moment to pray. Thank the Holy Spirit for his provision. Notice that not only does the Holy Spirit deposit his fruit individually, but as he does, they build upon, reinforce, and sustain each other.

Listen for and lean into any words the Holy Spirit wants to share with you.

Having laid a solid foundation for union with God, the next three fruit form the foundation of our relationship with others.

"Do not seek revenge or bear a grudge against anyone among your people, but love your neighbor as yourself. I am the Lord."
– Leviticus 19:18

Patience

If you're like me, patience is something you struggle with. This is especially true in today's fast-paced, instant response, microwave, coffee/meal to order on the go, *"gotta have it now"* world. The union of the sin of self with The World.

Patience is built upon and enabled by the three pillars the Spirit has already used to establish your steadfast relationship with God: love, joy, and peace.

Think about it.

When your heart is secured in love, joyful in the abiding presence of that love, and at peace in the assurance of that reality, isn't it much easier to be patient? Patient with your children? Patient with that screwball at work? Patient with the technology that isn't working as you expect? Patient in bumper-to-bumper traffic? Or patient with your spouse as they step on your wounded heart yet again?

> *"As for [the seed that fell] in the good soil, they are those who, hearing the word, hold it fast in an honest and good heart, and bear fruit with patience."* – Luke 8:15 ESV

Kindness

After patience, the Holy Spirit bestows kindness. It's hard to be kind, both to yourself and others, when you're stressed and overwhelmed. When everything around you appears to be set against you. Yet when we are grounded in love, confident in joy, resting in peace, and established in patience, is there any way *not* to be kind?

Kindness is the ultimate act of selflessness, of putting others first. But kindness flows not from acknowledgment of a clever saying or your own striving to be so. Kindness flows from rest. The rest that is formed through the enabling fruit we have already been given.

> *"He has told you, O man, what is good; and what does the Lord require of you but to do justice, and to love kindness, and to walk humbly with your God?"* – Micah 6:8

Goodness

Out of the overflowing abundance of the fruit already imparted, the Holy Spirit now establishes goodness. At some point in our lives, most of us men in the church have been told that our goal is to be good. Like the Army, "*God is looking for a few good men.*" But goodness is not something we can make happen or strive for. The goodness provided by the Holy Spirit becomes innate in us, a component of our DNA—tov. We become men fully capable of performing our design and purpose in creation. The harvest multiplying in the world exponentially.

> "*I myself am satisfied about you, my brothers, that you yourselves are full of goodness, filled with all knowledge and able to instruct one another.*" – Romans 15:14 ESV

Pause Again

> *Let this soak in and pray.*
>
> *Lord Jesus, continue to transform me by the work of the Holy Spirit depositing in me the Fruit of the Spirit. Thank you for the process that changes me and makes me a new creation. A man able to be all that you created me to be. Amen!*
>
> *Listen for and receive his response.*

Now we turn our gaze to the last three *Fruit of the Spirit*. It is these fruit that the world sees and marvels at. It is this fruit that overflows into the world and makes those around us ask, "*How can this be?*" This is the physical evidence in the world of environments that flourish. The question to which Peter encourages us to have a ready answer.

> "*...Always be prepared to give an answer to everyone who asks you to give the reason for the hope that you have.*"
> – 1 Peter 3:15

Faithfulness

As we continue our journey, we become faithful. Not because of what we have done or accomplished along the way, but because God, in his very nature, is faithful. And so, because we are created in the image of God, his innate faithfulness flows to us by the work of the Holy Spirit. Faithfulness, in union with the previous fruit, is birthed, nurtured, and fulfilled in us.

Faithful. We become so because he is.

> "*Your steadfast love, O Lord, extends to the heavens, your faithfulness to the clouds.*" – Psalm 36:5

> "*His master said to him, 'Well done, good and faithful servant. You have been faithful over a little; I will set you over much. Enter into the joy of your master.'*" – Matthew 25:23 ESV

Gentleness

As we near the end of our journey, because he has made us loving, joyful, peaceful, patient, kind, good, and faithful, we become truly gentle. Not out of force of will or empathy, but because of the unmoving foundation the Holy Spirit has built in us. Gentleness is our new nature. You are gentle because of the work of the Holy Spirit in you. You are no longer directed or controlled by fear and anxiety. They have no power or influence over you, and so you are simply gentle.

> *"Be completely humble and gentle; be patient, bearing with one another in love."* – Ephesians 4:2

> *"And the Lord's servant must not be quarrelsome but kind to everyone, able to teach, patiently enduring evil, correcting his opponents with gentleness."* – 2 Timothy 2:24–25a

Notice how the Fruit of the Spirit is entwined. Love, Joy, Peace, Patience, Kindness, Goodness, Faithfulness, and Gentleness.

Self-control

The impartation of the fruit of the Spirit concludes with self-control. The ability to be master over one's flesh and will. It is in self-control that you manifest Jesus to the world. It is in self-control that you live subject to the will of God—Father, Jesus, Holy Spirit. And it is by the Holy Spirit's work in you through his imparted fruit that you live a self-controlled, abundant life.

> *"A man without self-control is like a city broken into and left without walls."* – Proverbs 25:28

> "For this reason, I remind you to fan into flame the gift of God, which is in you through the laying on of my hands, for God gave us a spirit not of fear but of power and love and self-control."
> – 2 Timothy 1:6–7

> "Older men are to be sober-minded, dignified, self-controlled, sound in faith, in love, and in steadfastness. Likewise, urge the younger men to be self-controlled." – Titus 2:2,6 ESV

One Last Word

The *Fruit of the Spirit* are deeply interconnected and masterfully interwoven. They build upon one another in growing measure until we are truly a *"new creation."*[152]

It is in and through this mysterious act of redemption and renewal, the impartation of the *Fruit of the Spirit,* that your tov heart is nourished. It is through the *Fruit of the Spirit,* alive and established, that you learn to live abundantly. Each *Fruit* building upon the other in increasing measure—interconnected, additive, and interwoven. And yet, the impartation of the *Fruit of the Spirit* is not *"one and done."*

Each fruit works to build, support, and encourage the others so that *"the Spirit himself bears witness with our spirit that we are children of God"*[153] and we are truly able to:

> "Do everything without complaining or arguing, so that you may become blameless and pure, children of God without fault in a crooked and depraved generation, in which you shine like stars in the universe as you hold out the word of life."
> – Philippians 2:14–16

May the *Fruit of the Spirit* well up within you as you live out the abundant life through your tov heart. The world is desperate for Jesus and so is in desperate need of abundant life flowing through you. Creating environments where life can flourish.

> *"To him who is able to keep you from falling and to present you before his glorious presence without fault and with great joy—to the only God our Savior be glory, majesty, power and authority, through Jesus Christ our Lord, before all ages, now and forevermore! Amen."* – Jude 1:24-25 NIV 1984

FIND AND BE A BELAYER

The job of a belayer is to keep the climber safe. Period.

TOV MARKER

A belayer's job is to keep a climber safe as they make their ascent. We are told in scripture to be a belayer for others. And it is crucial that we find belayers for ourselves as we live from the tov heart. Ascending to the abundant life Jesus came to give.

A belayer's primary responsibilities include catching falls, providing tension on the rope, and managing slack in the rope. All providing for the climber's safety.

When a climber slips, the belayer, using a belay device, stops them from falling. Or, when a climber needs to take a break, the belayer can take slack out of the rope and lock the rope so the climber can rest, hanging in place without falling.

During a climb, the amount of slack in the rope is critical. It is the belayer's responsibility to ensure there is enough rope. Allowing for efficient movement and, if there is a fall, reducing the climber's risk of hitting the ground, outcrops, or other climbers. Too much slack and the climber can fall too far, risking injury to themselves or others. Too little slack and the climber is hampered in their climb and their ability to ascend.

Clear communication between the climber and the belayer is crucial to avoid confusion and redundancy. Both confusion and redundancy can lead to errors in action and judgment. Both of which can be disastrous for the climber, the belayer, or both.

As you walk with God in the fullness of your tov heart, you must both find and be a belayer. You must find and be part of a group of men who have each other's backs. Who encourage and support each other, and, when necessary, can call each other out.

I won't kid you, true belayers are hard to find. They are built out of relationship and a shared understanding of the Gospel and a deep walk with God. This has been one of the greatest struggles in my life as a Christian.

Don't get me wrong; I have friends, people who care for me. But a friend is not necessarily a belayer. Friends are close, but a belayer is closer still. He is someone who knows your story, understands your gifting, and is willing to stand in the gap for you when you can't stand on your own.

You must also be a belayer, managing another's ascent to abundant life with God in the context of their story and gifting. Recognizing that their climb is different from yours and must be managed as if their life depends upon it. Because it does.

> *"Above all, love each other deeply, because love covers over a multitude of sins."* – 1 Peter 4:8

> *"And let us consider how we may spur one another on toward love and good deeds."* – Hebrews 10:24

> *"Do not let any unwholesome talk come out of your mouths, but only what is helpful for building others up according to their needs, that it may benefit those who listen."* – Ephesians 4:29

> *"...encourage one another and build each other up, just as in fact you are doing.... And we urge you, brothers and sisters, warn those who are idle and disruptive, encourage the disheartened, help the weak, be patient with everyone."* – 1 Thessalonians 5:11,14

> *"Do nothing out of selfish ambition or vain conceit. Rather, in humility value others above yourselves, not looking to your own interests but each of you to the interests of the others."*
> – Philippians 2:3–4

> *"Carry each other's burdens, and in this way you will fulfill the law of Christ."* – Galatians 6:2

> *"We who are strong ought to bear with the failings of the weak and not to please ourselves. Each of us should please our neighbors for their good, to build them up....May the God who gives endurance and encouragement give you the same attitude of mind toward each other that Christ Jesus had..."* – Romans 15:1–2,5

Your mission, should you choose to accept it, is to find and be a belayer. Your tov heart needs encouragement and support as you journey into abundant life. And you need to offer the same to others on the same journey.

One of the most beautiful and powerful things I have found is that as I belay, I am belayed. And as others belay me, I belay them.

This is not something you have to make happen. If you are walking with others through your tov heart, it just does. This is the way of the Kingdom of God. The way of the tov heart.

PET PEEVE

"Now we know that whatever the law says it speaks to those who are under the law, so that every mouth may be stopped, and the whole world may be held accountable to God." – Romans 3:19 ESV

TOV MARKER

Accountability is a deadly concept in the Western church that has corrupted men's relationship with God. In what used to be called "accountability groups" and "accountability partners" it is an attempt at behavior management. An attempt to keep men in line and "make" them good. But we are never told in scripture to be accountable to another person. We only become truly good, tov, through the work of God in our hearts. We are only accountable to him. No one else.

A sinister and deadly infection has spread through the Western church. It has corrupted much of the evangelical church and is especially prevalent in men's ministries. The infection of accountability.

The center of many men's ministries has become accountability. Man to man, as manifested in what used to be called "accountability groups" or "accountability partners."

I was steeped in 1980s Christianity that used accountability groups as a tool of behavioral management to keep guys in line. But there is a problem. Broken men do not create unbroken men. We are all broken vessels and if we attempt to maintain our "goodness" and manage our behavior through our own striving, we will absolutely fail.

To offer grace, the intention was good. The offer of older, more mature Christians to lead and foster newer ones. Unfortunately, not through discipleship but through sin management. Men telling men to be good.

Abundant life can only be lived through union with God. The tov heart where a man's story and gifting are redeemed in the context of God's love. Goodness, behavioral change only occurs as the result of a choice and the resulting healing and restoration of the heart. Not the other way around. And heart change only occurs through the work of God—Father, Jesus, Holy Spirit. And, it must be chosen. As we've seen, redemption is the work of God AND we must say yes to the work.

Man to man accountability does nothing to change a man's heart or bring him closer to God. But it does provide a way for a man to justify hiding from the work of God he so desperately needs. As long as he shows up to meetings, admits he's broken, and says he's sorry he's good to go. For a little while.

Nowhere in the Bible are we told to be accountable to each other. Even when we are reminded to not cause another to sin, the resulting punishment is not managed or dispensed by man but by God himself and him alone. [154]

Even our leaders, when they fail in their mission or calling, are not accountable to their congregations or ministry members. Yes, there may be consequences that the congregations may need to dispense. But their ultimate accountability is not to their human sheep but to God.

> *"Obey your spiritual leaders, and do what they say. Their work is to watch over your souls, and they are accountable to God."*
> – Hebrews 13:17a NLT

Now, yes, we've seen in previous sections, that we're instructed to encourage, support, strengthen, teach, and guide one another. To carry one another's burdens and cares. And to intercede mightily in prayer for one another. But we are never, ever told to be accountable to another person. And we are never told to make or allow another person to be accountable to us.

The idea of one person being accountable to another is both unbiblical and destructive to the work of God in a person's life. The place of God being replaced by man.

For the one under accountability, the place of the omniscient, omnipresent God of the universe is replaced by a frail, imperfect, sinful human being prone to misunderstanding, confusion, and the consequences of their own sin.

For the one providing the *"accountability,"* they have, in their own arrogance and pride, assumed the holy, righteous position of God, exchanging a perfect relationship for an imperfect one.

Every accountability group or partnership I have seen or experienced in the church has failed and failed miserably. You're lucky if they last a month. Remember, you can run from man but not from God—Father, Jesus, Holy Spirit. And most men will run.

You can choose not to go to an accountability group or stay connected with an accountability partner. But once you say yes to God, you cannot escape his work in your life, no matter how painful or embarrassing it may be.

No matter what else God is doing in your life, if you say yes to him, he is growing you up, maturing you and there is nowhere to run. Nowhere to hide. Nowhere you cannot be present to the one who truly sees you, knows you, and loves you beyond your wildest hopes and dreams.

> *Before a word is on my tongue you, Lord, know it completely. You hem me in behind and before, and you lay your hand upon me....Where can I go from your Spirit? Where can I flee from your presence? If I go up to the heavens, you are there; if I make my bed in the depths, you are there. If I rise on the wings of the dawn, if I settle on the far side of the sea, even there your hand will guide me, your right hand will hold me fast. If I say, "Surely the darkness will hide me and the light become night around me," even the darkness will not be dark to you; the night will shine like the day, for darkness is as light to you.*
>
> – Psalm 139:4–5,7–12

PART SIX

EPILOGUE

CHAPTER 13
REPRISE

"Ask and it will be given to you; seek and you will find; knock and the door will be opened to you. For everyone who asks receives; the one who seeks finds; and to the one who knocks, the door will be opened."

JESUS OF NAZARETH
MATTHEW 7:7–8

FAILURE REDEEMED

"Repent, then, and turn to God, so that your sins may be wiped out, that times of refreshing may come from the Lord," – Acts 3:19

TOV MARKER
Confession time. I had an opportunity to bring life to a situation and I didn't. Not in the moment, not when it was needed most. But the tov heart is resilient and, in the Kingdom of God, it's never too late.

Recently I had an opportunity to make life flourish. A close friend of my wife had a gift for another friend that we were going to ship out. Originally, we were going to meet her at church to do the transfer but, as it turned out, we had to meet her at her home. When we arrived, she and her teenage son had just been in a small parking lot car accident. No one was injured, just some broken taillight plastic and scraped, dented fenders.

She was stressed and shaken, her son was withdrawn and silent. It was the perfect time to step in to create an environment where life could flourish. But I didn't.

I should have pulled them aside. Prayed over them. Brought the Kingdom of God and the love of Christ Jesus between them and the other party. The cross and blood of Christ against the spirits of anxiety and fear, anger and frustration, diminishment and desolation. Called on the Holy Spirit to provide strength, comfort, and peace. That is what I should have done. What God has taught me to do. Ask, seek, and knock.

But I was dealing with my own "stuff." The details don't really matter but I totally didn't do what I have been "preaching" in this book. I didn't ask, seek, or knock. I didn't create an environment where life can flourish. I got caught up in my own struggles and I was looking in and not out.

By the time we got home, I could feel in my soul that something was wrong. I went through the rest of the day with that nagging sense of disquiet. By the end of the day, I knew what was wrong and repented to God. But I didn't know how to respond in the earthly, physical situation—after the fact. I was thinking to myself, tempted by the Enemy, remember he's always in our failures to put his spin on it, *It's too late. Nothing you can do about it now.* But that is not how God works. In the Kingdom of God, it's never too late.

As is usual for me, the intervention of the Holy Spirit took place as I slept that night. My dreams were fitful and unremembered but when I awoke, I had direction. I knew what I needed to do. It's part of the mystery I have learned to be comfortable with and to lean into.

I texted Debbie's friend and told her I needed to speak to her and her son. Not urgent, there were some things I needed to say. We will get together tomorrow.

What will I say? I will give them a glimpse into purpose—into creating environments where life can flourish. I will ask their forgiveness for not doing that in the moment of their need. And I will offer it then.

How it turns out really doesn't matter. Their response is not up to me. What matters is that I continue to learn and grow. I may not "get it right" every time, but I can choose to live deeper into what God has given.

Deeper into my purpose. Deeper into union with God and others. Deeper into the tov heart.

We are not perfect and sometimes we drop the proverbial ball. But remember, we can pick it up and continue to run. In the Kingdom of God, it's never too late.

> *"Therefore, since we are surrounded by such a great cloud of witnesses, let us throw off everything that hinders and the sin that so easily entangles. And let us run with perseverance the race marked out for us, fixing our eyes on Jesus, the pioneer and perfecter of faith. For the joy set before him he endured the cross, scorning its shame, and sat down at the right hand of the throne of God. Consider him who endured such opposition from sinners, so that you will not grow weary and lose heart."*
> – Hebrews 12:1-3

REPRISE

LOOKING BACK TO GO FORWARD

"We need never shout across the spaces to an absent God. He is nearer than our own soul, closer than our most secret thoughts."
– A.W. Tozer, *The Pursuit of God*[155]

TOV MARKER

At the end we go back. Back to where we started. Ask, Seek, and Knock. It is to Jesus we turn but not for what we believe we want but for his will for us and a partnership in what he is doing. In every situation, good or not. In joy or in sorrow. In hope or in fear. Jesus leads us back to himself … the way, the truth, and the life.

Turn your heart and eyes back to the beginning.

As we wind up this part of the journey, I want to leave you with something useful. Something you can sink your teeth into, so to speak, that's more than just a witty "ism" or a list of "to-dos." As I listen to God, he has brought me full circle. Back to the beginning of the book for the end.

We started with the idea that I still have much to learn. And while that is still true, I have learned a bit more, and it may be the most important thing I ever say.

Matthew 7:7-8 has been part of my Christian vocabulary for half a century. But today it resonates with fresh meaning and divine purpose. Until today, this passage has been about me. Ask for what I want. Seek the things I desire. Knock on the doors which are closed to me. Ask, seek, knock. Simple, yes?

I am only now seeing this passage as the relationship model it is and the way we are to pray. The way we find union with God—Father, Jesus, and Holy Spirit. Especially when the circumstances of our lives turn upside down or have become easy and blessed.

This passage is two parts "What?" and one part "How?"

Jesus first tells us to ask, and it will be given to us. In the context of my Western evangelical story, the "it" has always been something I wanted. He then tells me to seek, and I will find what I am looking for. Lastly, he says to knock, and the door of opportunity will be opened to me.

But today, the focus has shifted away from me and something to him and nothing. Not nothing in the sense of emptiness or void but nothing in the sense of what I have yet to see and experience.

In the struggles and challenges, in the unknown, and in the abundance, he tells us it is him we are to ask, him we are to seek, and him who will show us the way.

But when life is easy and "going well," we tend to pull away from God. It's our natural, fallen proclivity toward self-reliance.

In this passage Jesus is showing us a way to live abundantly through the tov heart. A way to live in and through himself when your world begins to fall apart or when it is blessed.

"*Ask and it will be given to you...*" is where it all begins. When you don't know. When the world around you shifts, tilts, and begins to crumble—ask Jesus about the "What?" When things are easy, blessed and you begin to coast—ask Jesus about the "What?"

We tend to speculate. To guess. To make up stories in our heads to interpret what we are experiencing. The problem with speculation is that it's never based on reality. So rarely, if ever, does it play out as we expect.

But Jesus knows. The all-knowing God of the universe knows what's going on and he's eager to share that knowledge.

Jesus, what is going on here? Listen, wait, be patient. Keep your eyes on him and ask repeatedly if you need to. Stress is never our friend, and it is hard to hear when we are fearful or anxious. So, be still[156] and be patient.

"Seek and you will find..." is where we ask the next question, the follow-up question. Clarity and comfort. Before we "rush the field" or push ahead with our own response to Jesus' initial answer, ask the next question. We don't need to "figure it out." He will lead.

Jesus, what would you have me do? Jesus, what should my response be? Again, keep your eyes on him, listening and patiently waiting for his answer.

Lastly, *"knock and the door will be opened..."* is where we ask "How?" Following our initial questions to clarify what is going on and what he wants us to do in response, Jesus tells us to knock on the door of how.

Jesus, how do you want me to do it? With your eyes on him, you lean even deeper into his will.

What's going on? What would you have me do? How do you want me to do it? Three questions that work together to provide divine clarity in the Lord Jesus Christ.

If we ask, seek, and knock. If we will keep our eyes on him. If we will be still and know that he is God. Two parts "What?" and one part "How?" This is the way[157] we connect with the will of God. This is the narrow gate[158] we enter when the earth is shaken, and the mountains are removed.[159] This is how we navigate the unknown and the blessing with the courage and confidence that brings peace.[160]

And, as we mature in our faith, our relationship with God changes. As our role of a beloved son shifts and changes over time with our earthly father, the same is true with our heavenly Father.

In the ideal earthly father-son relationship we are the beloved, the apple of our father's eye. As we grow and mature, we take on the role of student and then apprentice. Learning from our father what it means to be a man and how to navigate life with his help and guidance. We may have our own children who become our beloved and we begin to teach, guide, and apprentice them. Life begetting life, exponentially. The lives affected may not necessarily be biological children. Friends, relatives, neighbors, friends of friends, etc. As far as the ripples of our lives run. Lastly, we take on our father's role in the world, head of the house, master of our own kingdom (little "k"). Our father's life overflows into us and then through us to create environments around us where life can flourish.

For many of us, me included, this is not our experience. However, this is exactly how our relationship with God the Father progresses. You are the beloved son. You are deeply and passionately loved. Through the tov heart, as you mature, you learn what it means to be a man and how to navigate your life with his help and guidance. We become students, disciples of Jesus. Learning from him the way of life, apprenticing moment by moment, day by day, year by year. Through us, the life of God—Father, Jesus, Holy Spirit—overflows into the world creating environments where life flourishes. Where others around you look at you and see you as a true son of your true Father.

Early on we spend most of our time asking, seeking, and knocking on behalf of ourselves. As we mature this changes to asking, seeking, and knocking on behalf of others—people and causes near and far. But, as our roots grow deep into the fertile soil of God's immense love, what we can dream and imagine seems to lack something. So, as we continue to mature, we begin to ask, seek, and knock to understand what God is doing and where he is going. To understand what he wants us to do in concert with that, and how he wants us to do it.

As the tov heart matures within you. As you step into fuller life with God. As the Father continues to hold and ground you in the fullness of his love. As Jesus, deeply indwells you with his life. As the Holy Spirit imparts, in greater and greater measure, the fullness of his fruit. You move more and more into the fullness of what it means to live a life as God's partner.

Beloved son, to apprentice, to disciple, to partner. And, in true God fashion, nothing given is ever lost. Even in partnership with God you are still his apprentice and disciple. And will always be his beloved son.

Ask, seek, and knock. Eyes on Jesus in every moment of every day through your tov heart. This is how you trust Jesus no matter what. This is how you live the abundant life.

So, as we part company for now, my prayer for you is an ancient one:

> "*May the Son of God, who is already formed in you, grow in you, so that for you he will become immeasurable, and that in you he will become laughter, exultation, the fullness of joy which no one can take from you.*"[161]

This is my desire for you as you journey with God into the tov heart. For you to live the abundant life Jesus promised. The life he will use to impact the world ... Godspeed Brother!

Amen! Amen!! Amen!!!

APPENDIX

GOING DEEPER

*Books and Apps are listed in alphabetical order.
Pray and let the Holy Spirit lead you where he wants you to go.*

BOOKS

The books listed here are in the library of my tov heart.

Beautiful Outlaw, John Eldredge

Becoming A King, Morgan Snyder

Diary of an Old Soul, George MacDonald

Knowing the Heart of God, George MacDonald

Letters to a Diminished Church, Dorthy Sayers

Letters to the Church, Francis Chan

Life Without Lack, Dallas Willard

Long Obedience in the Same Direction, Eugene H. Peterson

Lord of the Rings Trilogy, J.R.R. Tolkien

Moving Mountains, John Eldredge

Renovated, Jim Wilder

Run with the Horses, Eugene H. Peterson

So You Don't Want to Go to Church Anymore, Jake Colson

The Chronicles of Narnia, C.S. Lewis

The Handbook of Spiritual Warfare, Dr. Ed Murphy

The Imitation of Christ, Thomas a Kempis

The Paradise King, Blaine Eldredge

The Shack, Wm. Paul Young

The Spirit of the Disciplines, Dallas Willard

The Way of the Heart, Henri J.M. Nouwen

The Wisdom of the Desert, Thomas Merton

The World's Last Night, C.S. Lewis

To Be Told, Dan B. Allender, PhD

Victory Over the Darkness, Neil T. Anderson

Waking the Dead, John Eldredge

Wild at Heart, John Eldredge

APPS

BibleProject, BibleProject

Lectio 365, 24-7 Prayer

One Minute Pause, Wild At Heart (Ransomed Heart)

Pray-As-You-Go, Grupo de Comumicacion Loyola SL

Wild At Heart, Wild At Heart (Ransomed Heart)

NOTES

Introduction
1. Redford, Robert, dir. 2000. *The Legend of Bagger Vance.* DreamWorks Distribution, LLC.
2. Stewart, Mary. 2003. *The Last Enchantment.* Harper Collins.
3. Genesis 3
4. Crosby, Stills, Nash, & Young. 1970. *Woodstock.*
5. J. R. R. Tolkien. (1954) 2015. *Fellowship of the Ring.* Vol. 1. Harper Collins Publishers Limited.

PART ONE: FROM SLOW DEATH TO ABUNDANT LIFE
Chapter 1: Slow Death
6. Peterson, Eugene H. 2010. *Praying with the Psalms.* Harper Collins.
7. Thurber, James. 1939. *The Secret Life of Walter Mitty.* London: Penguin Books.
8. Hill, Napoleon. 2008. *The Law of Success.* Penguin.
9. Eldredge, John. 2008. *The Way of the Wild Heart.* United States: Thorndike Press.
10. Eldredge, John. 2009. *Fathered by God.* Thomas Nelson.
11. Scott, Emma. 2019. *Someday, Someday.* United States: Emma Scott.
12. Mann, Michael, dir. 2004. *Collateral.* DreamWorks Pictures.
13. Mangold, James, dir. 2010. *Knight and Day.* 20th Century Fox.

Chapter 2: Choosing Life
14. Eldredge, John. 2010. *Walking with God: Talk to Him. Hear from Him. Really.* Nashville: Thomas Nelson.
15. Eldredge, John. 2006. *The Way of the Wild Heart: A Map for the Masculine Journey.* Thomas Nelson.

16. Luke 2:19
17. John Eldredge, Podcast, 2012 https://libguides.csuchico.edu/c.php?g=414275&p=2823093
18. https://www.howstuffworks.com/hsw-contact.htm. 1970. "Why Is Water Vital to Life?" HowStuffWorks. 1970. https://science.howstuffworks.com/environmental/earth/geophysics/water-vital-to-life.htm.
19. Bernard of Clairvaux. AZQuotes.com, Wind and Fly LTD, 2024. https://www.azquotes.com/quote/649841, accessed October 29, 2024.
20. Philippians 4:7
21. Psalm 51:10-12
22. Eldredge, Blaine. 2023. *The Paradise King*. Blaine Eldredge.
23. John 16:33
24. Philippians 4:12
25. Philippians 4:13
26. John H. Stammis. Trust and Obey, *The United Methodist Hymnal*, No. 467

PART TWO: THE HEART OF EVERYTHING
Chapter 3: Awareness of the Difficult

27. McGrath, Tom, and Eric Darnell, dirs. 2005. *Madagascar*. DreamWorks Pictures, Paramount Pictures, FilmFlex.
28. John 14:16
29. Psalm 51:10
30. Eldredge, John. 2016. *Waking the Dead: The Secret to a Heart Fully Alive*. Thomas Nelson.
31. John 17:20-23

NOTES

Chapter 4: Finding Your Way

32. Jimmy Buffett. AZQuotes.com, Wind and Fly LTD, 2024. https://www.azquotes.com/quote/434168, accessed October 31, 2024.

33. Ken Jennings Quotes. BrainyQuote.com, BrainyMedia Inc, 2024. https://www.brainyquote.com/quotes/ken_jennings_423472, accessed October 30, 2024.

34. Eldredge, John. 2011. *Wild at Heart Revised and Updated*. Thomas Nelson.

35. Muller, Wayne. 2000. *Sabbath: Finding Rest, Renewal, and Delight in Our Busy Lives*. New York: Bantam Books.

36. Reitman, Ivan, dir. 2014. *Draft Day*. Lionsgate.

37. Frost, Robert. 2017. *The Road Not Taken*. Thunder Bay Pr.

38. Vasarhelyi, Elisabeth Chai, and Jimmy Chin, dirs. 2018. *Free Solo*. National Geographic Documentary Films.

39. ISPO. 2022. "Alex Honnold: First Free Solo Climber on the El Capitan | ISPO.com." www.ispo.com. August 26, 2022. https://www.ispo.com/en/people/alex-honnold-first-free-solo-climber-el-capitan.

40. Proverbs 18:24

41. Schaeffer, Francis A. 2020. *True Spirituality*. Crossway.

Chapter 5: Unconsidered Ascents

42. Edmund Hillary Quotes. BrainyQuote.com, BrainyMedia Inc, 2024. https://www.brainyquote.com/quotes/edmund_hillary_104652, accessed October 30, 2024.

43. John 7:38

44. Acts 17:28

45. Eldredge, John. 2024. "The Future of Wild at Heart." Wildatheart.org. June 23, 2024. https://wildatheart.org/podcasts/wild-at-heart/the-future-of-wild-at-heart.

46. Ezekiel 47:12

47. Ephesians 3:16-19
48. Genesis 1-2; Luke 19:10 NIV 1984
49. Matthew 13:23
50. John 5:5-9
51. Luke 18:35-42
52. Matthew 6:9-13
53. Blaise Pascal. 1972. *Pensées*. Paris: Librairie Generale Francaise.
54. Psalm 139:14
55. Proverbs 4:23
56. Matthew 11:28
57. Peterson, Eugene H. 2019. Run with the Horses. InterVarsity Press.
58. Chan, Francis. 2018. *Letters to the Church*. David C Cook.
59. Ephesians 3:16-19
60. Philippians 4:11-13
61. Philippians 4:7
62. Philippians 4:13 NLT

PART THREE: DISCOVERING GOD'S TOV HEART
Chapter 6: God The Gardener

63. Matthew 14:25-33
64. Matthew, 7:7-8
65. Lewis, C S. 1994. *The Magician's Nephew*. Vol. 1. New York: Harpercollins.
66. Schmidt, Ray. 2010. *In My Heart*.
67. Matthew 6:33
68. Romans 12:2
69. Ephesians 3:16-19
70. Hebrews 12:1-2
71. John 17:21-23

NOTES

72. Hebrews 6:19
73. John 10:10
74. Luke 9:51

Chapter 7: Sowing Tov

75. Heslop-Harrison, John. 2024. "Germination." In *Encyclopedia Britannica*. https://www.britannica.com/science/germination.
76. Genesis 1:28-29
77. John 17:20-23
78. John 7:38
79. Morgan Snyder, www.becominggoodsoil.com
80. Conan Doyle, Sir Arthur. 2015. *The Complete Sherlock Holmes*. Sterling Publishing Co, Inc.
81. Jenkins, Dallas, dir. 2021. *The Chosen, Season 2, Episode 2*. Lionsgate Television.
82. Ephesians 3:20
83. Luke 1:19
84. Revelation 20:11
85. Acts 2:28
86. Psalm 16:8-11
87. Psalm 139:7-12
88. John 14:16-17
89. John 14:8-9
90. John 14:18-19
91. Luke 15:11-31
92. 1 John 3:16
93. 1 Corinthians 2:9-16, Romans 8:12-17, Romans 15:13; Galatians 5:22-23
94. John 10:10

PART FOUR: AWAKENING THE TOV HEART
Chapter 8: God Math

95. Blaise Pascal. 1972. *Pensées*. Paris: Librairie Generale Francaise.
96. Scott, Ridley, dir. 2005. *The Kingdom of Heaven*. 20th Century Studios.
97. Allender, Dan B. 2005. *To Be Told: God Invites You to Coauthor Your Future*. Colorado Springs, Colo.: Waterbrook Press.
98. Meyers, Nancy, dir. 2026. *The Holiday*. Universal Pictures, Columbia Pictures, Sony Pictures.
99. Matthew 11:29-30
100. Baker's Dictionary of Biblical Theology, https://www.biblestudytools.com/dictionary/redeem-redemption/
101. John 19:30
102. Lewis, C S. 1994. *The Magician's Nephew. Vol. 1*. New York: Harpercollins.
103. Jenkins, Dallas, dir. 2022-2023. *The Chosen, Season 3, Episode 7*. Lionsgate Television.
104. Isaiah 61:1
105. Luke 14:28, NLT
106. *Ibid.*
107. *Ibid.*
108. Psalm 139:14
109. Proverbs 16:18
110. John 1:1-5
111. Eldredge, John. 2016. *Waking the Dead: The Secret to a Heart Fully Alive*. Thomas Nelson Publishers.
112. John 17:23
113. Chapman, Brenda, Simon Wells, and Steve Hickner, dirs. 1998. *The Prince of Egypt*. DreamWorks Pictures, Universal Pictures.
114. Stokes Mitchell, Brian. 1998. *Through Heaven's Eyes*.

NOTES

115. John 10:10
116. Jenkins, Dallas, dir. 2019. *The Chosen, Season 1, Episode 4*. Lionsgate Television.
117. Irenaeus, *Adv. Haer.* 4.20.7, trans. Robert M. Grant, *Irenaeus of Lyons*
118. https://wildatheart.org
119. Eldredge, John. 2018. "Work of Christ." *Wild at Heart*. October 23, 2018. https://wildatheart.org/rhplay/series/audio/work-christ.
120. Luke 15:4-7
121. Eldredge, John. 2016. *Walking with God*. Thomas Nelson.
122. Willard, Dallas. as quoted by Snyder, Morgan. 2013. "Who Are You Becoming? - Become Good Soil." *Become Good Soil*. October 9, 2013. https://becomegoodsoil.com/2013/10/09/who-are-you-becoming/.

Chapter 9: Farming Tov

123. Tyldum, Morten, dir. 2016. *Passengers*. Columbia Pictures, United International Pictures, Sony Pictures Releasing.
124. 1 John 1:9, Acts 3:19, 1 John 2:12, Acts 10:43, Colossians 1:14, Romans 6:23, Romans 8:1
125. Ezekiel 47-1-12, Revelation 22:1-2
126. Reinhold Niebuhr Quotes. BrainyQuote.com, BrainyMedia Inc, 2024. https://www.brainyquote.com/quotes/reinhold_niebuhr_121403, accessed November 29, 2024.
127. Ephesians 4:26-27
128. Jenkins, Dallas, dir. 2022-2023. *The Chosen, Season 1, Episode 1*. Lionsgate Television.
129. Clive Staples Lewis, and Walter Hooper. 1988. *The Grand Miracle and Other Selected Essays on Theology and Ethics from God in the Dock*. New York: Ballantine Books.

PART FIVE: GUARDING THE TOV HEART
Chapter 10: Required Nourishment

130. *Ibid.*

131. John 15:5

132. Allender, Dan B, and Tremper Longman. 1994. *The Cry of the Soul: How Our Emotions Reveal Our Deepest Questions about God.* Colorado Springs, Colo.: Navpress.

133. Marilla Cuthbert, *Anne of Green Gables*, Film, 1985.

134. Brooks, David. 2016. *The Road to Character.* New York: Random House.

Chapter 11: Understanding the Opposition

135. Lawrence, Francis, dir. 2013. *The Hunger Games: Catching Fire.* Starz Entertainment Corp.

136. Wikipedia Contributors. 2019. "Fog of War." Wikipedia. Wikimedia Foundation. September 20, 2019. https://en.wikipedia.org/wiki/Fog_of_war.

137. Fuqua, Antoine, dir. 2016. *The Magnificent Seven.* Columbia Pictures, Sony Pictures Releasing.

138. St. John of the Cross, Precautions; Thomas Aquinas, Summa Theologica; The Council of Trent, Sixth Session, Decree on Justification; The 1549 Common Book of Prayer, Baptism.

139. Pascal, Pensées

140. Genesis 19:17

141. Felder, Don, Don Henley, and Glenn Frey. 1977. *Hotel California.* Bill Szymczyk.

142. Ephesians 6:12

Chapter 12: Belayed & Belaying

143. Cox, Steven M.; Kris Fulsaas, eds. 2009. *Mountaineering: The Freedom of the Hills* (7 ed.). Seattle: The Mountaineers. ISBN 978-0-89886-828-9

144. Francis A. Schaeffer, *A Christian Manifesto*

145. Psalm 1:1-3, 121, 91

146. 1 Chronicles 15:34

147. 2 Chronicles 7:14

148. Revelation 22:20

149. "Belay Device." 2021. Wikipedia. May 24, 2021. https://en.wikipedia.org/wiki/Belay_device.

150. Deuteronomy 31:6

151. Romans 8:21

152. 2 Corinthians 5:17

153. Romans 8:16

154. Romans 14:10-12

PART SIX: EPILOGUE
Chapter 13: Reprise

155. Tozer, A W. 2015. *The Pursuit of God: The Human Thirst for the Divine*. Chicago: Moody Publishers.

156. Psalm 46:10

157. John 14:6

158. Matthew 7:13-14

159. Psalm 46:1-3

160. Philippians 4:4-7

161. Isaac of Stella as quoted by Renovaré. 2015. "Renovaré | How to Celebrate - Adele Calhoun." Renovaré. 2015. https://renovare.org/articles/how-to-celebrate.

ACKNOWLEDGMENTS

So many people to thank ...

First my amazing wife, Debbie. Your heart for others, patience with me, and love for Jesus have worked with God to make me the man I am and the man I am becoming.

There are many who have influenced this content, the sages quoted, the writers and directors who, unknowingly, provided illustrations, along with the many men and women who have informed my journey into tov. Thank you.

I am also forever grateful for the support, encouragement, correction, and love of my intercessors and allies. Tim Hayes, Dean Nikodemski, David Ballard, and Richard Miller. God has used our conversations, your challenges, and your heart and love for me and Jesus to inspire my love of God and others in and through the tov heart. You are my true belayers. Iron sharpens iron, Brothers! Iron sharpens iron. I am looking forward to sharing the best wine we've ever tasted at the wedding feast of our King!

Godspeed!

ABOUT THE AUTHOR

Ray Schmidt is an adventurer seeking the God of the universe in every aspect of life. A former Chief Information Officer and technology executive, he is now a mentor coach, author, and speaker at Invested Stories, the company he created to help others navigate the ancient path to abundant life with Jesus. Ray, his wife Debbie, and their four cats reside in North Myrtle Beach, South Carolina.

For more, visit InvestedStories.com.

www.ingramcontent.com/pod-product-compliance
Lightning Source LLC
Chambersburg PA
CBHW070138100426
42743CB00013B/2750